Create A Life You Love

10 Healthy Habits to Transform Your Life Now

Chantal Cox, MAEd

ISBN: 978-0-5784-68536-3

START YOUR JOURNEY HERE

In my experience, the best way to get the most out of a nonfiction book is to implement and take action as you go.

To help with this, I have created FREE resources for each chapter.

Download Your *FREE* **Resources** at www.ChantalsCreations.com on the Book Resources Page.

If writing a book is part of your journey to ***Creating a Life You Love***, check out this free webinar to learn the 3-step blueprint I followed to make my dream a reality.

Access Your *FREE* **Webinar** at http://bit.ly/2RclKrB

Dedication

*This book is dedicated to the brave souls willing to step out of your comfort zone and do the hard work to **Create a Life You Love**.*

You are not alone on this journey. Welcome!

Contents

A Note to The Reader

If you're serious about changing your life, you'll find a way. If you're not, you'll find an excuse.

~ Jen Sincero

You were not created to live a mediocre life consumed by stress, anxiety, and self-doubt. However, only you have the power to create an extraordinary life and accomplish goals you never dreamed possible. Like many of us, you may be asking, "How am I supposed to do that? I can barely keep up with the laundry."

The awesome thing is that you have made the first step. You have opened yourself up to **Creating a Life You Love** simply by reading this book. By intentionally implementing the incredibly simple practices outlined within these pages, you will begin embarking on this beautiful adventure.

As a teacher, blogger, YouTuber, and someone who herself continues on this amazing life journey, I've read or listened to hundreds of hours of top-rated self-help books. I've whittled down various tips from many leaders in the self-help field and I've developed and introduced these simple lessons into my own daily routine, adapting them to fit my "real life" circumstances. The positive impact has been so astounding that it has become my mission to help teach others, and you, how *Creating a Life You Love* can be done without spending countless hours trying to filter through hundreds of pages.

This book is designed to be a quick read, offering strategies you can implement immediately. It will take you through exercises to practice new skills that help set you up for lifelong success. In a matter of a few days, by following these easy to apply practices, you'll begin to develop the ability to radically transform your health, happiness, relationships, and career.

My profession as a special education teacher has provided me with the skill of simplifying content into practical, bite-sized pieces, designed to help anyone from beginner to intermediate to become successful. Each chapter will focus on the importance of allowing ourselves grace when we inevitably stumble, being consistent, and finding the courage to just get started no matter where you are in your life. This is a book written by an imperfect person for imperfect people. We will focus on striving for progress, not perfection.

In my own personal journey, I've gone from someone with such low self-esteem and negative self-talk that I have literally covered mirrors, refusing to look at myself. I've entered multiple negative relationships, allowing myself to be a doormat. I've been on so many antidepressants and anti-anxiety medications at one time that my liver practically shut down. There was even a particularly low point in my life when chunks of my hair had fallen out due to my not having the coping skills I needed to deal with the stress and anxiety of life.

It wasn't until six months out of a physically, emotionally, and mentally abusive marriage that I figured out that life did not have to be so hard. This started the multi-year journey that leads me to write this book today. I believe everything happens for a reason, and through my past experiences and lessons I learned the hard way, you won't have to learn these lessons on your own.

I don't wish for you or for anyone to be like I was for so many years, hearing but not listening to words of wisdom and advice from people who truly cared about me. At the time, I was too stubborn and unwilling to look at life from another perspective. When someone would suggest something as simple as starting a gratitude journal, I would politely smile and say it sounded like a good idea, but inside I was thinking, "Who has time for that? You have a perfect life. It's easy for you."

The reality was, as the saying goes, as long as I kept doing the same things, I was going to get the same results. It wasn't until I hit my physical and emotional rock bottom that I was ready to pay attention and try something new. This is not an easy process and it takes work, but YOU are worth the work. YOU are worth the journey of self-improvement.

Whether you want to move carefully, making small changes in baby steps, or if you feel ready to embark on a complete personal overhaul, the simple practices you are about to learn from this book will help you change the way you show up to your life every day. I am so excited to welcome you to this beautiful, transformational journey!

It's time to radically change your perspective and begin to *Create a Life You Love*.

Chapter 1
Make YOU a Priority

*Almost everything will work again if you
unplug it for a few minutes, including you.*

~ Anne Lammott

Why is it so easy for us to jump through hoops
and bend over backward helping family, friends,
and coworkers? We give generously of our time
and energy without a second thought. Then when
it comes to taking care of our own needs,
suddenly there is a massive time shortage, and
we feel guilty or selfish for even thinking of it.

For years I was given the common advice of:

- "You have to put on your own oxygen
  mask before you can help anyone else
  around you."

- "You can't pour from an empty cup."

I would smile politely while thinking cynically to myself, "Yeah, well these lesson plans aren't going to write themselves, the lawn isn't going to mow itself, and the laundry certainly isn't going to do itself. So take your oxygen mask and empty cup and shove it!"

Admittedly, I was not in a good headspace back then and could not step back and appreciate the big picture. I remember being 24 years old, in my second year as a special education teacher, and I had the brilliant idea of enrolling in a master's program. After all, I was single and had no children. Now was the perfect time to be as selfish as I needed to be with my time. I could easily pull all-nighters writing papers and it would be a snap to attend a class once a week until 10 p.m. after a full day at work.

It all seemed like a good idea. However, if you are an educator or know an educator, it is common knowledge that teaching is definitely not a 9-to-5 gig. Many teachers eventually get into the groove and have systems in place that help them have time for a life outside of work. Unfortunately at that time, I was definitely not one of those teachers, and my inexperience proved that I was not quite as efficient with my time as I thought. I would aim to get to school by 6:30, a full two hours ahead of the required start time, and stay until 8 most nights. This exhausting practice kept my head above water...barely. Compound that schedule with the classes and homework from the master's program I had been so excited to add to my workday, and it brings us to my first scary realization that maybe I did need to listen to the well-meaning advice of others.

Time to Take Notice

As I was getting ready for work one morning, a flash of something light-colored caught my eye on the top of my head. I have dark hair and there was a large white spot on my scalp. Upon further investigation and with the help of my smartphone camera, I found a bald spot a little larger than a quarter. Completely bald. Smooth. Not a whisper of even the tiniest hair. I was shocked. *How in the world did that get there? Did I somehow get ringworm?* My confusion quickly turned into all-out panic. *Do I have a brain tumor that is pushing on my scalp from the inside, making my hair fall out?* Please remember that I am not a medical professional and had not had a stress-free day or a good night's sleep in over a year, so this was no time for logic.

As I stood there alone in my bathroom, I continued to spiral with more panic-driven questions. *Who would ever date a bald girl? I'm going to die single, alone, and bald! How was I going to show up to work looking like this? Work? Oh no, work! I am supposed to be getting ready for work.* Luckily since I was typically about two hours early, I was not going to be "late" by contract standards. I tried headbands and a variety of hairstyles before deciding to use bobby pins to secure hair from my bangs area to go up and over the bald spot, also known as a comb-over, which is not exactly every 24-year-old girl's dream hairstyle.

Feeling highly self-conscious and barely holding it together, I headed to work. One benefit of being a special education teacher is that you usually are assigned paraprofessionals to help cover student needs. At that time in my career, I was blessed to be working with four fabulous women who knew my workaholic tendencies, and me, all too well. When Deana came in, she gave me a genuine smile and said, "Love what you did with your hair girlfriend!" I burst into tears.

I then showed her the reason for the new hairstyle, and she politely pointed out there was another smaller spot behind my right ear that I had not even noticed. More tears. After the school nurse confirmed it did not look like ringworm, I made an appointment with my primary care physician, who had no idea what could be causing it or how to treat it. I became obsessed with checking my head for more bald spots, convinced it was spreading and soon I would be completely bald.

Fortunately, one of my other fabulous paras, Josefina, had a stepdaughter who happened to be a dermatologist in town. I made an appointment to see her and discovered that what I had was called alopecia areata. It is an autoimmune disease where your immune system attacks your hair follicles. It can be genetic and/or can be triggered by severe stress. To my knowledge, no one in my family has ever even heard of this ailment, so this was a pretty clear sign that I needed to make some changes, fast!

Time for Changes

I was apparently not as self-sufficient and strong as I pretended to be, so I began to put systems in place and seek help from others. I realized that my lawn wasn't getting mowed regularly with my busy schedule. Every time I scheduled a block of time on a weekend to mow, it would inevitably rain. This was an easy stressor to eliminate. I found a laid-off aircraft worker in a Craigslist ad who was happy to come and mow every other week. For me, this little luxury was absolutely worth adding to my household budget.

Diet was next on the agenda, meaning not just concern with my weight, but with lack of nutrition in general. I had been living off of whatever could be delivered or ordered at a drive-thru window. If the budget was tight at the end of the month, it was common that my dinner would consist of a bag of popcorn, pretzels and a cheese stick, or a stale hotdog bun with a melted piece of cheese on it. I was 40 pounds overweight and clearly not giving my body the nutrients it needed to function successfully. I've heard that diets don't work unless you do them for yourself, so I made the commitment to make myself a priority. I started shopping at budget-friendly grocery stores and meal prepping so I would have healthy options readily available when the busy schedule and stress kicked in. I was inspired by a documentary on Netflix called *Fat, Sick, and Nearly Dead* by Joe Cross, so I bought a juicer and started having two "Mean Green" smoothies per day.

In addition, I *finally* listened to the advice of my mentor, Christy. She lived nearby and would text me if she happened to be driving past the school and see my lone car in the parking lot late into the evening. "Go home! It will all still be there tomorrow!" I learned to prioritize my tasks, got better at delegating, and discovered how to work my classroom schedule so that even though there were students in my room at all times of the day, I had planning time and, dare I say, even a lunch! Gone were the days of discreetly nibbling on a protein bar while instructing a small group of students. It was time to realize that not taking a break to take care of my needs throughout the day meant my students were not getting the best version of me. They deserved better than the hungry, exhausted, stressed out version of me. I was finally done pretending everything was under control.

Another Example

Maybe you are thinking to yourself, my life is a lot more complicated than yours was at age 24. Trust me, I get it. Ten years later, my life has changed too. I do, however, find myself back at a place where I am again single with no kids, so let me share another example that might resonate with you.

My mom is pretty freaking awesome. This is not the first time I have written about her being a hero and role model to me. Many of my high school essays and college papers speak of how her brave choices shaped me and helped create an amazing life where we lived in multiple countries and traveled the world.

Growing up, I watched as she slowly developed the understanding of how to make herself a priority. At some point in my early years, she left the Army (I told you she was awesome), and after a brief stint working at an office job, she took the most important job role of her lifetime and decided to become a stay-at-home mom. She was no ordinary housewife. She was always busy as a room mother, church nursery worker, PTO member, Girl Scout leader, and as an Odyssey of the Mind coach. Pretty much anything and everything she could be involved with, she was. However, she was usually not just involved, she led or even started many committees and projects.

For example, when we were living in Panama, it was not enough to be our Girl Scout leader, she became the lone Troop Committee Chairperson.

She was flown to New York for training and then was in charge of Girl Scout Cookie sales for the entire country of Panama. When we moved to Luxembourg, the fact that Girl Scouts had not been established was unacceptable. So of course, she did what needed to be done to organize and initiate a new troop.

Not only did she take on the many pressures of being super mom, but meanwhile, my dad was working his way up the ranks in the Army, and she was frequently the "hostess with the mostest." She would host high-ranking officials and diplomats for dinner and attend fancy events as the Commander's Wife. To this day, she still has multiple sets of Villeroy & Boch dinnerware, though their current guests on their 99-acre farm tend to dine on disposable, or at least dishwasher-safe plates.

Time to Take Notice

To the outside world, and even from my view as her daughter, she seemed indestructible and unstoppable. She was always up for any challenge and wouldn't hesitate to pull an all-nighter to decorate a beautiful cake shaped like a bunny rabbit for my sister's birthday or to finish sewing our matching purple Halloween princess costumes. When I was 8 years old, I remember finding it odd that she always seemed to be sick and lose her voice on Christmas morning, though I didn't spend much time thinking about it after seeing the massive number of presents Santa magically delivered while I was sleeping. Oh, and did I mention the homemade cinnamon rolls to get our tummies nice and warmed up for the lavish feast that she had also lovingly prepared for us?

I was oblivious to the pattern that after large, stressful events such as helping to organize the Toys for Tots gift drive, she would inevitably get a bladder infection and be in severe pain for several days. I don't think any of these things connected until I was in 8th grade and we were living in Luxembourg. There was a large military holiday dinner two hours north in The Netherlands. My dad had gone up earlier for meetings, and she was going to drive up on her own and meet him for the event. I stayed back and babysat all of the kids from the various family friends who would also attend the dinner.

It was late and I had put the kids to bed when the phone rang. This was well before the convenience of cell phones and I was not sure if I should answer the landline phone at the house that was chosen as the babysitting location for the evening. Luckily they had an answering machine that allowed you to screen calls, listening to the message as the caller recorded it. I heard my mom's voice saying that if I could hear her, pick up. I obliged thinking nothing of it, she was just checking in, as mothers often do.

She was not, however just checking in. She was calling to say that it would be a little bit later than planned when she returned that evening. On the drive home, she had hit a patch of black ice and had lost control of the Volvo she was driving. I learned the details later, how her car had careened across the multiple lanes of the autobahn several times, and then had narrowly missed a semi-truck before crashing head-on into a cement barrier at over 70 miles per hour. Fortunately, all of the safety features that Volvo advertises worked perfectly. Multiple airbags deployed and the engine dropped down instead of crashing into the car cabin, which would have crushed her legs, if not worse. Miraculously, she walked away with a nasty bruise where her body was thrown into the seat belt and her face was red and felt sunburnt from where her face and the airbag collided.

Time for Changes

This event grabbed my family's attention in a big way. In the days following, my mom shared that she had not been feeling well and had thought about not going to the dinner. She spoke about how she should have listened to her gut feeling and stayed home to take care of herself. She had been spending so many years putting everyone else's needs above her own and she made a decision: Things were going to change.

About six months later we moved to the Washington D.C area. I started high school and my sister was now in third grade. It was time for mom to start reclaiming her own identity outside of "Chantal and Michelle's mom" and "Bob's wife." She got a part-time job at Ross Dress for Less and found a running buddy. At some point, in an unsuccessful attempt to keep my sister interested, she joined a dojo and started learning Taekwondo, a form of martial arts. While my sister lost interest and dropped out not long after, mom stuck to it. My mom turned into a board breaking, sparring, all-around Taekwondo rock star.

My mom finally decided to make herself a priority. When she stopped pretending every-

into how to set specific goals in Chapter 8, but for right now think about what your current practices are and if you are willing to add time to your routine to focus specifically on self-care.

Here are a few simple self-care practices you can begin incorporating right now.

- Take 5 slow, deep breaths-in through your nose and out through your mouth

- Go for a walk

- Take a bath

- Pet a cat or dog

- Stand up and stretch, reaching all the way to the ceiling, then all the way down to the floor

- Put on your favorite upbeat song and dance like no one is watching

- Laugh-whether it is with a friend, child, or due to a funny YouTube video, take a minute to genuinely laugh

- Light a candle and just be still and quiet, watching the flame dance for at least 60 seconds

- Look in the mirror and say something kind to yourself

- Reflect on something you are grateful for

- Gain perspective by asking if what you are stressing over will still be as important in 5 hours, 5 days, or in 5 weeks, months, or years

These exercises can be done immediately and in a short amount of time, yet can have positive effects that last for hours. I challenge you to try a few of these strategies over the next couple of days. Take note of how you feel before and after. There is no time like the present to get started. If you set a goal to practice self-care twice a day and you only manage to get to it once, allow yourself grace and try again tomorrow. We are human and imperfect; the important thing is to begin again and not to just give up all together.

To download a printable version of these simple self-care ideas, visit the Book Resources Page at www.ChantalsCreations.com.

* * *

Final Thoughts

I am happy to report that after multiple rounds of steroid injections into my scalp, my hair did eventually grow back. The treatment was not pleasant or cheap, so I highly recommend taking care of yourself prior to your body providing a reason for you to do so.

According to the National Alopecia Areata Foundation (NAAF), approximately 6.8 million people in the United States and 147 million worldwide have or will develop alopecia areata at some point in their lives. If you or someone you know is showing symptoms, seek the advice of your doctor or dermatologist. You can also visit the NAAF website at www.naaf.org for helpful resources.

Chapter 2
Be Grateful

Gratitude is the healthiest of all human emotions. The more you express gratitude for what you have, the more likely you will have even more to express gratitude for.

~ Zig Ziglar

As I started out on my personal development journey, I began to devour all of the self-help books I could get my hands on. I decided to not only read, but to use time commuting in my car to listen to audiobooks. This dramatically increased the number of books I could consume in a short amount of time.

In the beginning, I would simply read or listen to the books and reflect on the words of wisdom. Then I started noticing patterns and asking myself questions. *Why would Brene Brown, John C. Maxwell, Zig Ziglar, and so many others all go on and on about the importance of gratitude?* For most other people, they probably would have gotten it while reading their first self-help book, but I will be the first to admit that I am not always the quickest to pick up on things. However, since they all seemed to be pretty emphatic regarding the importance of it, I decided I should pay attention.

At the time, I was juggling many responsibilities and had full and long days consisting of work, a walking club after hours with co-workers, coursework for a second master's level program, and then one to three hours of Latin and ballroom dance classes four nights a week. This meant I was getting home around 9:30 most nights. Keeping track of an actual handwritten, pencil to paper gratitude journal was not going to be a reasonable expectation for me. I imagined myself saying, "Whoops, forgot my journal at work, guess I'll catch up tomorrow," which would inevitably turn into never.

This was several years after my experience with the episode of stress-induced hair loss as mentioned in Chapter One. Yes, my days were still long and still over-scheduled. But something had changed. I began to put systems, boundaries, and self-care activities in place and was actually beginning to live the best version of my life up to that point. Taking my current lifestyle into account, I planned the best way for me to incorporate a daily, written gratitude journal. I became determined to find a way that could be successfully sustained for the long term. I chose to use the OneNote program, which was already synced across my phone, iPad, and laptop. I committed to writing a minimum of three things I was grateful for every day with no repetitions. I also set a reminder on my phone to go off every morning, so I would remember to keep up with it.

The Practice of Gratitude

The first few days, the novelty of it all made it fun and exciting, but I didn't necessarily have an immediate, life-changing experience. I knew that just like all other healthy habits, consistency would be the key, so I plodded along this new path. I enjoyed taking a few minutes each day to reflect on three things to be grateful for and after a few weeks, I noticed my perspective was beginning to shift. I always felt naturally inclined to be pessimistic, and I had a long history of depression and anxiety. However, suddenly I was beginning to see things in a new light.

I recall my extreme annoyance that the apartment complex where I was living scheduled the sprinkler system to operate every morning right as I was leaving for work. I grumbled to myself about how the sidewalks were not in need of water and someone should really re-calibrate or re-time these infuriating water blasters.

After keeping my gratitude journal for a few weeks, one morning I walked out and made it to my car before the sprinklers started. I was overcome with joy, excitement, and gratitude. I was thrilled to add this to my list for the day. Then it struck me: If I had not been focusing on being grateful, how would I have responded to this same situation? Would I have even noticed? I had taken my first steps into learning *The Practice of Gratitude.*

As the days and weeks went on, there were more and more times where I caught myself being giddy with joy over small things that I probably would have taken for granted had I not been focusing on and truly practicing gratitude. Even when unfortunate things happened, I was able to find something in the situation to be grateful for. For example, when my car was involved in a hit and run in a parking lot the Sunday evening before Martin Luther King Jr. Day, I'm sure you might imagine that my initial reaction was not gratitude. However, over the following days, I found myself writing these entries in my journal:

I am Grateful For:

- The holiday; so I can spend the day figuring this out without taking time off from work

- Car Insurance

- My emergency fund; so I could easily pay the insurance deductible (Thank you, Dave Ramsey)

- Excellent customer service from the car rental agency, which picked me up in a rental car from the auto body shop

- The use of a rental car

- Excellent customer service at the auto body shop

- Getting my car back as good as new

Prior to beginning *The Practice of Gratitude*, I guarantee that the few days it took to resolve this issue would have been fraught with negativity and a downward "woe is me" spiral. This led to another "Aha!" moment: life is too short to be so negative. Dwelling in negativity does no good and changes nothing regarding the actual problems or circumstances we're facing. We get so wrapped up in our own thoughts, that the lens through which we see life dramatically impacts our perception, and our perception becomes our reality. If I had perceived the hit and run as the worst thing to ever happen to me, it would have been. However, my perception wouldn't prevent the hit and run. It still would have happened. The circumstance remains the same; we can only control our reaction to it. The best way to change a negative perception is through *The Practice of Gratitude.* It's a learned skill, finding what we can be grateful for, even in the most negative situation, and choosing to focus our minds on that.

Research on Gratitude

Over the past several years, gratitude has gained popularity as a study topic for neuroscientists and psychologists. In fact, Dr. Robert A. Emmons from the University of California, Davis, and Dr. Michael E. McCullough from the University of Miami did a ten-week study on gratitude where they split the study participants into three groups. The first group was asked to write about things they were grateful for throughout the week. The second group wrote about their daily irritations or things that had upset them. The third group just wrote about events that had affected them with no directions as to if it should be positive or negative.

At the end of the ten weeks, the participants from the first group were more optimistic and felt better about their lives overall. It was also noted that they exercised more and had fewer trips to the doctors' office than those in the other groups. It is worth noting that this was incorporating a weekly gratitude journal rather than a daily one. Imagine the impact a few minutes a day could make on your life.

Another study done by the National Institutes of Health (NIH) used a Magnetic Resonance Imaging (MRI) scan to examine blood flow to various sections of the brain when study participants focused on feelings of gratitude. The participants who showed more gratitude had higher levels of activity in the area of the brain known as the hypothalamus, which controls essential bodily functions such as eating, drinking and sleeping. This area of the brain also influences your metabolism and stress levels. They concluded that by improving your levels of gratitude, you could experience an increased effect from exercise, improved sleep, decreased depression, and fewer complaints of aches and pains.

The final research information I will mention in this section is from neuroscience researcher Alex Korb, Ph.D. In his book titled *The Upward Spiral: Using Neuroscience to Reverse the Course of Depression, One Small Change at a Time*, he explains the relationship between gratitude and happiness. He shares that feelings of gratitude activate the regions of the brain that are associated with the release of dopamine and serotonin. These are neurotransmitters associated with promoting initiative, enjoyable social interactions, mood regulation, appetite, and sleep. Many antidepressants such as Prozac work by boosting the production of serotonin. Korb explains that when you make a conscious effort to be grateful, it engages your brain in what he calls a "virtuous cycle." Basically, once you start on this path of gratitude, your brain starts to look for more and more things to be grateful for. How awesome is that?

Now by no means am I telling you to flush your antidepressants and start a gratitude journal. First of all, that's bad for fish and other creatures living in the river and sea. Please dispose of medications safely. Secondly, getting off anti-depressants is a personal choice, and should be done under the care of your doctor. I am simply sharing this information to illustrate that there is research that supports scientific and biologic value in positive psychology practices such as maintaining a gratitude journal.

Your Turn

We all live busy lives, but this seems like a no-brainer. A gratitude journal takes minimal time, effort, or money. Yet, it can have an immensely positive impact on your life. If you do nothing else differently after reading this book, I challenge you to at least try a simple gratitude journal for one month. If after that month, you see no positive change in your life, drop it like a bad habit. However, I suspect it will surprise you, and will become something you will choose to continue.

In order to implement this insanely simple strategy, follow these steps:

1. Decide how you will document your gratitudes

- This could be electronically, in a notebook, or as my friend Lisa does, on a Post-It note each morning and hang it on a Gratitude Board in your office. This is a great visual for when you need a little boost of positivity throughout your workday.

2. Gather the needed materials

- Download your app of choice, get a journal or notebook specifically for your gratitudes, buy sticky notes, whatever it takes to remove any and all excuses on why you cannot follow through.

3. Set your goal

- How many? Determine the minimum number of gratitudes you want to write down each time, common numbers are three or five. Remember this is a minimum amount, you can always do more.

- How often? I recommend daily, however, it does not have to be daily if that seems too overwhelming when you are getting started, but like any healthy habit, you will experience results quicker if you are consistent and do it more frequently.

- When? I prefer to start my morning off with this practice as it sets the tone for my day. Others prefer to reflect on their day and write their gratitudes before bed. Choose what is best for you. Perhaps it is midday during your lunch to give your afternoon a boost.

- Where? Decide where you will practice this new habit and then set up a conducive environment. For example, if it is the first or last thing you are going to do each day, perhaps you want to keep your journal on your bedside table.

4. Set reminders

- You can use your phone, calendar, a sticky note on your bathroom mirror or coffee pot, or whatever system works best for you.

5. Get started

- There is no time like the present, just jump in and start.

6. Be consistent

- Aim to be consistent with this practice every day, but allow yourself grace and kindness if you forget. Just hit your reset button the next day and keep going.

7. Reflect

- Set up a time to reflect on the changes you are noticing. It could be weekly or any other period of time that is appropriate in your situation.

You may also choose to use the following sentence structure to write an intention statement that you can post where you will commonly see it and repeat it. Really dig into the details and envision yourself following through with the task. Imagine how you will feel incorporating this new routine. This statement can be as brief or lengthy as fits your personality.

Template:

I write down *How Many* gratitudes every *How Often*. I do this *When Where. Any additional Information.*

Example:

I write down *3* gratitudes *every day.* I do this *every morning while sitting at my sunny dining room table with my morning coffee. I enjoy this daily practice because it helps set the tone for my entire day.*

Notice how it is written in the present tense. You can use this idea to help you stay focused and accomplish any new habit or practice you are wanting to incorporate into your life.

That's it, you're on your way to **Creating a Life You Love** with your first super simple strategy. You have all the tools you need to be successful with the first step. Prior to reading the next chapter, I recommend that you take time right now to follow the steps and set up the journal method you've selected. In order to assist you with this, I've compiled some simple self-care ideas.

To download a printable version of these simple self-care ideas, check out the Book Resources Page on www.ChantalsCreations.com.

Chapter 3
Bust Out of Your Comfort Zone

Life will only change when you become more committed to your dreams than you are to your comfort zone.

~ Billy Cox

I sat in my dark apartment living room sipping on Sprite, waiting for my headache to go away as I reflected on the events from the previous evening. I had opted to join my group of close friends for a nice dinner and then an evening out on the town to celebrate New Year's Eve. For many years, this had been the usual ritual. I had a fun new sparkly shirt, and I was not worried about the fact that this time around I would be one of the only single people in the group.

Everything was going as planned until the clock struck midnight and it became painfully evident that I was the only one without a partner with whom to share a New Year's kiss. The massive amounts of alcohol that had been consumed over the last few hours did not help me keep my emotions in check. I suddenly became the girl that all friends dread being stuck with. My emotional breakdown led to my friend April calling our mutual friend who had opted to stay home. "Kayla, you need to come to get Chantal now!"

The following morning I was embarrassed, hungover, and pondering how in the world this was my life. My goal had been to be married with children by the age of thirty. How was I sitting alone in an apartment reflecting on the whirlwind of my life over the last six months since my divorce? Oh, and I happened to be thirty at the time, although fortunately, my short-lived marriage did not involve us having children.

I indulged in my pity party for a few hours as I binge-watched Netflix and ordered Chinese food. When Netflix annoyingly asked, "Are you still watching?" I wanted to throw the remote at my TV. I felt faced with a decision. I could easily push "Continue" and waste away the rest of my day. Fortunately, something inside of me yearned for more. I had come to a crossroads.

Time for Changes

Over the course of the last year, I had gotten married, and then seven months later, divorced. I was proud of myself and so thankful for my support system for helping me get out and stay out of my physically, mentally, and emotionally abusive marriage to a self-diagnosed Narcissist. I had escaped what was rapidly escalating into a fatal outcome. I should be living my life to the fullest, after all, I was given a second chance at life and had a fresh new start.

I was familiar with the saying that the definition of insanity is doing the same thing over and over again while expecting different results. As I pondered this, I asked myself, *"What were the results I was hoping for? What's my next step? What am I going to do differently?"* I certainly was not currently living a life that I loved.

I grabbed a notebook and started jotting down things I always said I would do but had never gotten around to doing. After my list was compiled, I read through it looking for a new goal; something that I could attain reasonably soon to pull myself up and out of this funk. I put a big star next to "Learn how to salsa dance," and opened my laptop. As fate would have it, there was a beginner's group class the following night. The website stated that no partner or experience was required.

I immediately blasted the information all over my Facebook page, asking, or more like begging, someone, *anyone* to come with me. Several people liked my status, and a few even commented that it looked like fun and they had always considered checking something like that out. At the end of the day though, there were no solid takers.

Stepping Out of My Comfort Zone

Through reflecting on my past patterns, I knew that I was a big chicken. In fact, when I was growing up, I was so self-conscious that when we were out as a family, my sister Michelle, who is six years younger than me, often had to accompany me to the bathroom because I was too scared to go alone. The social anxiety of walking alone through a restaurant to find the bathroom seemed worse than just waiting until someone else needed to go. Being somewhat self-aware, I knew if I wanted to give myself a chance to succeed at dance lessons, I needed to put something in place so that I would not chicken out so easily. I decided to notify my closest friends and family by publicly displaying my new goal on Facebook. I asked a few of them to check in with me afterward, hoping that the fear of admitting that I had not gone to the lesson, and having to fess up to what a weenie I was, would be enough to hold me accountable.

I'll be honest, I talked myself out of it, and back into it, at least twenty times throughout that day. However, somehow I made it there. It was a cold, dark, slushy January evening. The small parking lot in front of the building was filled. I was not familiar with the neighborhood, and the side street down the block was not well lit. *"This is it, this is how I die. Just trying to learn how to salsa,"* I thought dramatically to myself.

I made it to the studio's front door and was warmly greeted by one of the owners, who welcomed me and shared that I could leave my shoes by the door. I looked down at my slush covered boots and thought, *"These are the only shoes I brought. Now what am I supposed to do?"* Nearing panic, I complied with his directions and then followed him to the back room where the salsa class was to take place. I was already beginning to regret being there and stood awkwardly in my socks when one of the other dancers walked over and introduced herself. She said she had happened to bring an extra set of shoes that I was welcome to borrow. I gratefully accepted her kind offer, and noted to myself that if I survived this experience, I would Google what kind of shoes one is supposed to wear when attending a dance class.

The details of the rest of the class are fuzzy, other than the fact that I was pretty sure I had two left feet. I apologized for messing up every two seconds, and discovered that the room was filled with some of the most patient, welcoming, and fun-loving people with whom I had ever had the pleasure to interact.

When I arrived home, I excitedly posted on Facebook about how awesome it was and tried to convince others to join me the following week. Still no takers, but I was proud of myself for following through, stepping way out of my comfort zone, and surviving. Maybe the next week would be easier.

Predictably, my social anxiety kicked in the following week as class was approaching. This time I had scrounged up an inexpensive, strappy pair of black heels that had been collecting dust in my closet. Feeling a little more prepared, I mustered my courage and entered the studio.

A surge of panic came over me. The previous week there were about twelve people, who all seemed to know each other, and it was a laid-back atmosphere. This week, the room was buzzing with over thirty people! Where had I gone wrong? I had checked and double-checked the studio's website and their Facebook page to be sure it was the same time and place every week and that no weird event was scheduled. When I saw the unexpected crowd of people, I wanted to turn right back around, walk to my car, and get out of there!

Instead, I took a deep breath, found an empty chair to change into my "dance" shoes, and my thoughts began the downward spiral. I knew these were not real dance shoes and surely one of these people was going to call me out at any minute for being a fraud. Then, the lady sitting next to me asked if I was here for the MeetUp. I stared at her blankly, my eyes beginning to burn with tears of embarrassment. "No, I came for the salsa class," I meekly explained. "Am I in the wrong place?" She was very friendly, explaining that there was an app called MeetUp, and she was part of a MeetUp group called "Explore Wichita" that was checking out a salsa dance class together. We chatted for a few minutes about what MeetUp was and it hit me, "You mean I can join a free app and do things like salsa classes with a group of strangers when my friends are too busy to hang out with me?!" I pulled out my phone and she helped me download the app right then and there.

Disclaimer: My friends are, and continue to be, amazing in so many ways. However, my life changed significantly when I moved back and filed for divorce. Their lives seemed to be moving on happily with their significant others, even with the responsibilities that come with being married and having a family. Marriage followed so quickly by divorce had been a traumatic series of events, and getting back to a normal life was a difficult adjustment for me. The last place I wanted to be was alone in my apartment.

I had been avoiding any dreaded alone time by frequenting a local dive-bar for karaoke with my new partner in crime, Kayla, who was in her early twenties and always up for shenanigans. It was a fun and predictably safe distraction, but definitely not a long-term solution, at least not one that matched with what I wanted for my future. As I scrolled through the MeetUp calendar on my new phone app, it became apparent that by stepping out of my comfort zone to show up for a dance class, I had stumbled across another fantastic way to begin to *Create a Life I Love*.

An Unexpected Transformation

Over the next several months my life went through a complete transformation. I continued with the beginner's salsa class on Tuesdays, then began staying for the intermediate class that followed. I attended a workshop for another Latin-style dance that I had never heard of called Bachata with the MeetUp group, and then started attending that class on Wednesday evenings. Since there was a large group class that rotated on a monthly basis, I began attending those classes too. One month we would learn a simple pattern for Rumba, then the next month it would be Cha-Cha, Waltz, Foxtrot, Tango, or some other type of dance. I was building friendships with the other dancers in the various classes and we started finding dance opportunities outside the studio. Latin Night on Fridays, a live cover band on Saturdays, Bachata Festival in Dallas, larger Latin Nights in Kansas City, or West Coast Swing Workshops in Oklahoma City. Dance became a significant part of my life, and I was losing weight without even trying.

When I wasn't dancing, I was attending MeetUp events and even began hosting a few events from time-to-time. We would go to the movies, we might check out Happy Hour at a local restaurant, or dance to a local band. We even went on a couple of out-of-state Float Trips. I was meeting other people who had gone through life events that changed their social circles. Many of us were divorced, but some were simply new to the area due to their job locations and were looking to get plugged in somewhere. There were also couples who just wanted to get out more and meet new people. It was nice to normalize my feelings of isolation and understand that the struggle to meet adult friends is a challenge for many.

Six months later, when my thirty-first birthday rolled around and marked the anniversary of the day I left my husband, my life had done a complete turnaround. To celebrate, I took myself skydiving. This experience had been on my bucket list for my thirtieth birthday, but I had been forbidden to do this by my now ex-husband. This was not only out of my comfort zone, but was my unequivocal proclamation of freedom. I was free to do what I wanted, whenever I wanted and no one could make me back down. I was now fully in charge of my life, and it felt awesome!

Your Turn

As Eleanor Roosevelt said, "Do one thing every day that scares you." I challenge you to take a few minutes to do the following activity. Divide a piece of paper into three columns and label them with the following headings from left to right. "What I Want to Do," "What is Stopping Me," and "My Plan."

Add as many items as you like and keep this list for yourself to use as a reference and as a reminder. I continually add to my list and have also added this piece to my daily journaling practice. I write what I've done that day that was out of my comfort zone. Your day-to-day practices do not have to be huge, courageous acts. You might do something as simple as trying a new restaurant rather than going to the same place you always go. What started for me as taking a simple salsa dance class led to unimaginably positive changes in my life. You can do this exercise on a piece of paper, or access a free template as part of the Free Resources Page on my website.

To download a printable version of these simple self-care ideas, check out the Book Resources Page on www.ChantalsCreations.com.

When you put yourself out there, you never know what doors it will open, so be consciously open to new opportunities. In the movie "Yes Man" starring Jim Carrey, his character decides to say "Yes" to everything after attending a self-help seminar. His whole life turns around as he experiences all kinds of transformational events such as getting a promotion and meeting a new love interest. This is a fictional comedy and he ends up realizing that too much of a good thing can cause you to lose your balance. However, what we can take from it is the message that by saying "Yes" when someone invites you to try something out of your comfort zone, it can lead to amazing things. You must still use your best judgment and don't put yourself in harm's way; unless it's in the form of skydiving, then have at it!

What you will find is that the more often you step out of your comfort zone, the easier it becomes. The first several dance classes and MeetUp events were preceded with hours of anxiety for me. However, this was also an opportunity to practice my positive self-talk, which we will cover more in-depth in Chapter Five. With consistent practice, over time, these activities became my new normal and are no longer scary.

I initially thought I would go to one salsa class and then go back to my normal life. I'd like to encourage you to not be satisfied by trying just one thing. Make stepping out of your comfort zone a regular exercise. As with every new experience, if you plan to do something and you feel that you've chickened out, be gentle with yourself. Commend yourself for having a growth mindset that is open to new opportunities, and then try again tomorrow. Reflect on what it was that caused you to avoid following through and put new plans in place to overcome that barrier. The hardest step is the first one, so just go ahead and take it. You can learn to *Bust Out of Your Comfort Zone*. And once you get started, who knows how your life will transform? I learned it myself: The Sky is the Limit!

If you are interested in MeetUp groups available in your local area, visit www.MeetUp.com or download the free MeetUp app available on the Android and Apple iOS store. You might meet new friends, you might have a life-changing experience, or it might just be that crucial first step that helps you ***Create a Life You Love***.

Chapter 4
Expand Your Mind Through Reading

Remember, you are the same today as you will be in five years, except for two things: the people you meet and the books you read. Choose both carefully.

~ Charlie "Tremendous" Jones

Being an educator, I consider myself a lifelong learner. I keep going back to school to expand my mind and further my professional development. However, on a teacher's salary, at some point it becomes impractical, and I must seek out other ways to challenge myself and to continually grow. What is it that challenges and pushes you? Are there specific areas in your life that you wish to improve?

I've always enjoyed reading, to the point that I would stay up way too late on school nights lost in a good book and then be exhausted at school the next day. However, once I entered my freshman year of college, reading became a requirement to complete papers rather than something done for pleasure. It wasn't until after I had finished my first master's degree that I was able to once again pick up a book to read just for pure entertainment.

While audiobooks have been around forever, it wasn't until they became so easily accessible through apps such as Audible that I realized the magnificence of what they had to offer. All of a sudden, I could power through an entire book on a road trip, not really wanting to get out of my car when I had to stop for gas, and arriving at my destination feeling invigorated and alive. When I started reading and listening to more and more books in the self-help genre, the journey to ***Create a Life I Love*** began to pick up pace and noticeably build momentum. The authors challenged me, making me reflect critically on where I was and where I wanted to be. I reached a whole new level of understanding as potential opportunities began to unveil themselves.

I read everything I could get my hands on. After all, I was a self-proclaimed "hot mess." Not just any old hot mess, I saw myself as a steaming pile of hot messiness. I longed to feel like my life was "put together" and be one of those people where everything seemed to fit together like a picturesque puzzle. Unfortunately, I seemed to be working from a garage sale puzzle box that was missing a few pieces. I knew I didn't get to this place overnight and it would take years of hard work to pull myself out of this hole in which I found myself. But I knew one thing for certain: I wanted, no I *demanded* more, and I was determined to find out how to accomplish this seemingly overwhelming goal.

One method I found to do this was to read words of wisdom from those who seemed to know what they were talking about. I had taken Dave Ramsey's *Financial Peace University* years ago and had jumped onto that bandwagon with full force, even briefly leading a small group through my church. I also had the opportunity to meet Mr. Ramsey in person at a leadership conference. My friend Megan and I were totally starstruck and acted like big nerds about it.

Dave (I'll pretend I'm on a first-name basis with him for a moment) frequently stresses the importance of seeking out successful people and then emulating what they do. He shares that the average millionaire reads at least one non-fiction book per month. Now, I have no desire to be a millionaire, but surely there has to be some logic to this theory of success being linked to strong reading habits. Perhaps this new step could help me on my journey to climb out of the mental and emotional mess I had created for myself.

Crash Course Into the Self-Help World

The first non-fiction book I read as part of this journey of self-improvement was, "Daring Greatly" by Brene Brown. I had seen a clip of her Ted Talk at a training I had attended. I was intrigued and had jotted her name down as someone to research later. Something about her authenticity spoke to me, and I wanted to know more about who she was and what else I could learn from her. I downloaded the book on Audible and started listening while commuting to and from work and while driving for work throughout my day.

I had enjoyed audiobooks prior to this but had mainly focused on fiction novels for entertainment purposes. I was amazed not only by how quickly I was able to power through her book, but by how her words were making me think, and were connecting with me on a different plane than my favorite fiction books ever did.

My car became my therapist's couch as I pondered her insights on shame, vulnerability, authenticity, and courage. *What would it look like if I began to Dare Greatly? What might I be able to accomplish if I got over the fear of failure? What if I stopped trying so hard to appear strong and was actually authentic and vulnerable?* These lessons were totally against everything I had been trying to do post-divorce. My motto had been that I was strong and had overcome the most challenging situation I hope I'll ever have to face. I would get angry at anyone who I perceived saw me or treated me as a victim. I was a *survivor* dangit!

Yet, as I listened to Brene tell her stories, in her own voice via her audiobook, I didn't judge her imperfections or mock her shortcomings. I connected with her and began to be more forgiving when thinking of my own flaws. *Successful people who write books, go on TED Talks, and get their doctorates aren't "real people" with "real problems" and "real flaws," are they?* In my disillusioned head, I saw her successes as unattainable for someone like me.

As I moved onto a second book from Brene Brown, "The Gifts of Imperfections," I was struck by something she said, "I now see how owning our story and loving ourselves through that process is the bravest thing that we will ever do." *Owning* my story? I'm sorry, what? I've gotten really good at hiding my story, running away from my story, and avoiding my story! Why would I want to *own* my story? This perplexed me and I did what I did best: I ran back to my comfort zone and moved right back to nonfiction audiobooks that were more related to my professional life rather than my personal one. However, years later, owning my personal story has become a valuable piece of my healing and growth process. Chapter 10 is dedicated to the importance of each of us learning to own our life stories.

I got back on the professional self-improvement journey but this time I focused on books geared towards leadership, productivity, and purpose. I had completed my Building Level Administration program a couple of years back and I was considering someday becoming a Principal or a Special Education Assistant Director. I knew at this point in my life and career I was not ready for such a big step, but I also knew that now was the time to focus on learning and growing so I would be prepared when the time came.

I powered through more John C. Maxwell books than I can list, and enjoyed reading the popular "Eat that Frog" productivity book. I also read an incredible account from John O'Leary in his book "On Fire" where he shares the story of how he was burned on one hundred percent of his body as a child and survived against all odds. For years he hid his scars and didn't talk about his story until decades later when his parents published a book recounting the ordeal and how it impacted their family. He did not want them to share the story and was unprepared when local groups started asking him to come and speak. Over the years he not only embraced his story but has used it to help inspire people all over the world. I began to wonder if my story would be helpful to others. I believe that all things happen for a reason but at that point, I hadn't quite figured out why my life had taken such an unpleasant detour.

A Personal Metamorphosis

I joined a health plan called Profile with two of my friends from work. I was on summer vacation and I was focused on healthy eating and walking three to five miles a day, occasionally breaking into a slow jog that most people could easily outwalk. Since I was not driving as much, I was listening to audiobooks on my walks. I started noting that the tips listed in the various books from various authors frequently had some commonality. I began to compile the multiple messages into a spreadsheet, partly because I'm a nerd and I love spreadsheets. I blame my dad, but at this point, my friends and co-workers see it as my quirk since they don't know him or his affinity for spreadsheets.

As I was evolving and changing, I was doing what everyone does these days, posting updates on my Facebook page. Pictures of my walks, positive quotes, and inspirational videos began to take over my page. As with many things in life, when you focus on improving one area, other areas start to improve too. Through implementing small changes, I was noticeably slimming down and becoming an all-around more positive and healthy person, and people close to me started taking notice.

I began to hear from family, friends, and co-workers who told me that a simple Facebook post inspired them to make a healthy choice, or reminded them to spend a minute being grateful. My nature as a teacher blended with my never-ending desire to read and learn led me to embark on the new adventure of starting a YouTube channel. I started producing short, inspirational videos to share the practices and habits I was developing and implementing. About a month into the YouTube project, the opportunity to write a book that would provide an in-depth look into this topic presented itself.

While I may never meet the amazing authors of the multitude of books I've read, I distinctly feel they were shaping me and mentoring me. I was learning and growing from their wisdom. It was not enough to simply read the books though. I had to analyze what aspects I could incorporate into my life and how to adjust the ideas to fit into my lifestyle so that I could practice these new habits successfully.

Throughout this book, I share the handful of habits that have helped me on my journey so far, but without expanding my knowledge through reading, I do not believe that any of this would have been possible. Reading is the foundation on which the healthy habits were built, and it's a daily practice I plan to continue for the rest of my life. The minute I feel I'm done learning and growing is the minute I'll likely be dead.

The Value of Reading

Think about some of the great influencers out there. Many of them have recommended reading lists or even book clubs. Dave Ramsey, John C. Maxwell, and Oprah just to name a few. Why would these highly successful leaders stress the importance of focusing on your personal growth and development through reading if they did not value its significance?

In 2009, Thomas C. Corley released a book titled, "Rich Habits: The Daily Success Habits of Wealthy Individuals" where he summarized his research on 1,200 wealthy people to see what habits they had in common. His definition of "wealthy" was someone with an annual income of $160,000 or more and a liquid net worth of at least $3.2 million. He found that not only do eighty-six percent of rich people enjoy reading, but they tend to stick to non-fiction books, typically in the self-improvement genre and autobiographies or biographies of other highly successful people. Sixty-three percent said they listened to audiobooks on their commutes. While Corley's study was focused on "rich people," and fitting into that category is not my goal, what rich people do is often what successful people do.

My definition of success for myself would be if I could someday look back on my life and feel confident that I made a difference. Growing up in Girl Scouts, when we went on field trips or visited any new location, we were often reminded to leave that place better than it was when we found it. If we met in a church basement and it had clearly not been cleaned in a while, we were not to stop at just picking up after ourselves. We were instructed to leave it cleaner than it had been prior to us entering as a thank you and as an act of service for others. I want to live my life in that way, and upon reflection, this ideology is tied into why I chose to go into education and why I now feel so passionately about embracing and sharing my story with others.

Your Turn

Think for a few minutes: What is your definition of success? Write out your definition and ways you can achieve it. Don't limit yourself to what you think you can accomplish today with your current knowledge, confidence, and skill set. In the words of Les Brown, "Shoot for the moon. Even if you miss, you'll land among stars!"

Refer to your list every few months and see how you have changed and how those goals are able to expand as you see more opportunities to grow and adapt. Find the overarching theme to your goals and begin seeking out non-fiction books and authors that write about this area of expertise.

Considering that you are reading this book, perhaps the next few sentences might be a bit like preaching to the choir. However, I encourage you to make reading part of your daily routine. With consistent practice, you can build the momentum needed to reach your goals more quickly. As you read, pair this daily activity with reflection. Reflect on how what you have read impacts you. If you'd like, you can even jot down a few key points from what you read that day. Be intentional with your growth. Growth doesn't just happen, we must consciously invite it to happen.

Perhaps you strive to be a better parent, educator, leader, or perhaps you just want to gain clarity on your life's goal and purpose. We are in an age where our ability to access knowledge is more abundant than ever. We can download and read or listen to a book with a tap of a finger on a phone screen at minimal cost. There are also resources called Massive Open Online Courses, shortened to "MOOCs," available to help expand our knowledge for free, or at least at low prices, and we can teach ourselves practically anything on YouTube these days.

Evaluate your learning style and pick the option, or options, that work best for you. I know many people who don't feel they can focus on audiobooks. They are visual learners and need to see the words to grasp them fully. Find what works for you, but begin expanding your mind today. You are already reading this book, but don't stop there. Begin to think about what your next book might be or what other ways you can incorporate ongoing personal growth and development on this journey to *Create a Life You Love*. There is no time like the present. Decide how you will expand your mind a little bit each day, and commit to it.

On my website www.ChantalsCreations.com, you'll find a page titled Recommended Books. This is where I review some of the books that are helping to shape me on this journey. I'll continue to update this book list as I continue to read and grow.

You can also check out my YouTube channel titled Chantal's Creations where I share tips from this book and others.

Chapter 5
Replace Negative Self-Talk

Your beliefs become your thoughts, your thoughts become your words, your words become your actions, your actions become your habits, your habits become your values, your values become your destiny.

~ Gandhi

Think about the last time you didn't meet your own expectations. Perhaps you didn't get to your workout, arrived a few minutes late to a meeting, or maybe you impulsively bought something that wasn't in your budget. If you felt regrets about your behavior, how did you deal with that? What words came immediately to your mind? If you are like many of us, your internal monologue can be quite malicious.

Now think of a time when a close friend or family member did one of those same things. What was your external dialogue to them? Most likely, you viewed these things as small indiscretions, and you probably encouraged them with grace and kindness. We would never imagine making hurtful, judgmental comments to another human being, particularly if they're feeling discouraged. Why are we so readily able to be so sharply cruel to ourselves?

As I reflect on my years of practicing negative self-talk, I can't come up with a logical reason why it was such a pervasive force in my life. I came from a loving, caring, supportive home where my accomplishments were frequently celebrated. My sister, who was raised in the same home, didn't seem to suffer from the overwhelming negativity that constantly clouded my thoughts.

I couldn't take a compliment and would argue with anyone who dared try to give me one. For as far back as I can remember, I would make a self-deprecating joke, referring to myself as the "brown daughter," overweight, or ditzy. It was like the character Fat Amy says in the movie "Pitch Perfect" when she is asked why she refers to herself as "Fat Amy." Her response, "So twig b*tches like you don't do it behind my back," not only elicited a laugh from me, but unfortunately, it rang true to that aspect of my life. If I could beat others to the punch; putting it out there that I was unworthy of love and attention, then I couldn't be hurt when anyone rejected me later.

The overbearing pattern of negative self-talk that was constantly screaming in my head led me to make poor choices. I had a mild eating disorder in high school. I was referred to as the "water girl" because I was constantly refilling my water bottle. The truth was, I was trying to trick my stomach into not feeling hungry because I was living on 200 calories per day and diet pills. I dated guys who reflected my negative perception of myself. If they were unkind to me, it was oddly comforting because it somehow validated my inner beliefs about myself and how I felt I deserved to be treated. I was fortunate to have a few gems sprinkled in among the guys I dated, but for the most part, I had a type. If they paid attention to me and confirmed what I already believed about myself, it was a perfect match. Writing about it now, I can honestly see how far I have come and I'm so grateful that I'm no longer trapped and controlled by my own negative thoughts.

I sincerely hope that you have not experienced this level of self-abuse and that you have a more balanced relationship with your self-talk. I am blessed to have people in my life who have helped me find the resources I needed to get through the hard work of retraining my thoughts. I only share that brief glimpse into my "steaming hot mess" psyche to help you realize that there is hope. However, if you feel your negative self-talk is beyond what the exercises in this chapter can address, I highly recommend that you seek help from a trained therapist. I have sought therapy a handful of times since my senior year in high school and will continue to do so if the need arises in the future. The habits and routines in this book can be helpful companions but are not intended to replace the treatment of a licensed professional.

Why Is This Critical?

You may be thinking that your self-talk is nowhere near the negative level expressed in the previous example. Your own self-talk practices might seem harmless; after all, no one can hear the words you think, so it can't possibly hurt anyone. Right? Wrong! Being stuck in a cycle of negative self-talk can have a lasting impact not only on your self-confidence but on what you will be able to achieve in your life. If you constantly tell yourself you're too dumb to finish that degree, too fat to get a date, unworthy of that promotion, etc., your negative beliefs will become your reality.

I believe that on some level, we all have an understanding of the cause and effect relationship between most things in our lives. We know that if we go to work, we get paid. If we don't go to work, we lose our jobs. If we eat healthy and workout, we will have more energy and become healthier. If we eat junk food and binge watch Netflix several hours a day, our waistlines will grow larger. Where is the disconnect when thinking of how cause and effect applies to our internal dialogue? How can we begin to understand that negative self-talk will negatively shape our reality?

One way to examine this is through the practice of goal setting. We can set goals for ourselves, but if negative self-talk tells us we won't be able to accomplish our goals, then it becomes a self-fulfilling prophecy, also known as *limiting beliefs*. Negative beliefs about ourselves may limit the goals we are capable of achieving, and negative self-talk is at the core of all this.

For example, perhaps you set a goal to lose 20 pounds, then immediately remind yourself that over the years, you've set a million weight loss goals and have never managed to stick to the plan. If this negative self-talk sounds familiar, then I have good and bad news for you. The good news is that the predictions you make for yourself will be correct. You won't stick to the plan, and you won't lose 20 pounds. The bad news is that your limiting beliefs and negative self-talk just stopped you from accomplishing an entirely achievable goal. We will dive deep into how to set specific, measurable goals in Chapter 8.

Your Turn

When I was growing up, I was not allowed to read the popular book series that all of my peers were raving about. When I was caught reading one of the books from the "*Goosebumps*" series, I received a stern lecture from the maker and enforcer of the rule, my Dad. He explained, "We can put good stuff in our heads, or we can put bad stuff in our heads." He lovingly wanted to protect me from filling my head with negative and scary thoughts, knowing that what I read would impact my thoughts long after I set the book down.

What do your internal thoughts say to you throughout your day? Are you allowing the good stuff about yourself to bounce around in your head all day, or has the bad stuff taken over and become your routine?

Regardless of where you are on this journey to **Create a Life You Love**, our thoughts can usually use a slight makeover. Whether we like it or not, our internal dialogue is running at all times. We can allow it to run unchecked and hope for the best, or we can decide to take charge. One way to begin retraining our internal dialogue is through the use of positive self-talk statements, also known as *Affirmations*.

The term "affirmation" can sometimes elicit mixed emotions. Some think of the humorous Saturday Night Live skit, *"Daily Affirmations with Stuart Smalley,"* and find it corny to look into a mirror to recite statements like "I'm good enough, I'm smart enough, and doggone it, people like me." You don't have to call them "affirmations" if you're not comfortable with that word, but we do need a way to rewrite our internal conversations. This process takes time and practice and can feel overwhelming. However, after poring over multiple books on this topic, I have worked it down to five, easy to follow steps.

Take some time to reflect on the areas in your life you'd like to improve. Common areas are health, money, career, and relationships, but you can choose anything important to you. It's helpful to write down your thoughts in a quiet, distraction-free environment as you go through the following activities.

Step 1: State Positively

Since we've learned that our thoughts become our reality, it is imperative that our affirmations be stated positively in order to manifest a positive outcome. If we say and think about how we do not want to go broke, we will unconsciously continue doing things that keep us broke. Write a list of the positive things that you want in your life. If your go-to internal thoughts are phrased in a negative way, try this exercise to help flip your thoughts into positive statements:

1. Draw a line down the center of a piece of paper to separate the page into two columns

2. On the left-hand column, write everything you DON'T want in your life

3. Go through your list line by line and flip your thought to a more positive statement listed on the right-hand column

Examples:

1. I don't want to be unhealthy---> I want to be healthy

2. I don't want to be broke---> I want financial security

3. I don't want to be single---> I want to be in a happy, healthy relationship

4. I'm tired of being sick and tired---> I want to be energetic and healthy

5. I don't want to nag my husband and kids ---> I want to enjoy and appreciate my family

6. I can't maintain this level of stress---> I want to relax and practice self-care

Once you've completed your list and you've flipped your thoughts to more positive statements, read through them and see if similar statements can be grouped together. During the next step of this exercise, I'd recommend starting with up to three items. Prioritize your statements and highlight the few you'd like to use for this next step.

Step 2: Use the Present Tense

Think back to your days in English class when terms such as past tense, present tense, and future tense were taught and practiced. When writing affirmations, it is essential that they are written in the present tense.

Think about it; we wouldn't use the past tense because what we've been doing is not what we desire to continue. If we use the future tense, it turns into a wish that might someday happen in the future. In this version of the Goldilocks story, we'll find that writing in the present tense is "just right." Phrase your statements as if they are already true. The kicker here is that we're learning to align our behaviors to match our present tense statement; the lesson of cause and effect. If we state that we are healthy, then it must be that we are demonstrating healthy habits and behaviors. When you find yourself ready to make an unhealthy choice, you can repeat your affirmation statement to help remind yourself that you are healthy and you make healthy choices. Your affirmation statement becomes the positive self-talk you've been waiting to hear.

Example:

- Future Tense to Avoid: I will be healthy

- Present Tense to Use: I AM healthy

Please note that when you state affirmations in the present tense, if you don't already believe it, the affirmation won't work. Self-doubts will creep right back in and take over your internal dialogue. To help combat this, when you state "I am healthy," and you hear your old, negative inner voice saying, "I wish I was healthy, but I just had a giant gourmet coffee with a million empty calories." Use your new, positive inner voice to firmly tell that negative voice to "Zip it!" Allow yourself grace and kindness as you restate your positive affirmation and reset your thoughts for the remainder of your day.

For someone like myself who was conditioned to believe the negativity I was feeding myself, it can be helpful to soften the beginning of your affirmation with an opening statement until you build your confidence.

Examples:

- *I am in the process of* creating a healthy life.

- *I am committed to* building financial security.

By adding "I am in the process of," or "I am committed to," you can still make a positive statement in the present tense while not having to fight the negative "Yeah, right" or the "I wish" arguments in your head.

Step 3: Focus on How You Will Feel

Imagine how you will feel once your affirmation *is* reality and include those emotions in your statement. It's helpful to spend time focusing on the "why?" of your affirmation. *Why* do you want to be healthy, prosperous, in a relationship, etc.? Maybe you want to be healthy to be around longer for your children and family. Maybe you want to live prosperously rather than worrying about living paycheck to paycheck. Whatever your "why?" statement is, incorporate how you will feel once you have attained your goal.

Example:

- I am in the process of creating a healthy life and I am overcome with joy now that I can keep up with my kids. I am so excited to watch them grow up and to know I'll be there for all of their milestones.

If we don't tie our affirmations back to our "why?" statements and elicit strong emotions, we'll just be making random, meaningless statements. Your statements give voice to your dreams, and with practice, your repeated affirmations will begin to evoke an encouraging, emotionally positive response from deep within your mind and heart.

Step 4: Practice

Our brain is a muscle, and just like exercising to prepare for a marathon, we must practice and train consistently if we want to see results. We can take a cue from Muhammad Ali who once said, "I figured that if I said it enough, I would convince the world that I really was, The Greatest."

To practice affirmations and positive self-talk, I personally love using the free "ThinkUp" app which you can download at http://thinkup.me/

or on the Apple and Android stores. You can browse their library of affirmations or create your own. Once you've selected a few that you like, you can record them in your own voice and listen to them on a loop. Part of my morning and nighttime routines includes listening to my affirmations. It has been amazing; the changes in my own perception of myself, my abilities, and the opportunities that have presented themselves to me since I started this practice. I firmly believe that the same opportunities were always there, but I was like a horse with blinders on, only able to see what my limited scope of vision allowed. It's mind-boggling how wonderful the world is once you remove your own blinders.

Step 5: Be Thankful

As you know by now, I am a big proponent of daily gratitudes. Now that you know how to write affirmations, I recommend that you incorporate a *Proof Journal* to document and be thankful for the abundance that comes your way. Since one of the areas I am personally committed to is creating a healthy life, I write down every time I get a compliment, make a healthy choice when presented with temptation, or reach a milestone on my health journey. When I'm feeling down and focusing on negativity regarding this goal, I read through my *Proof Journal* and it helps reset to more positive self-talk.

As you spend time focusing on how your affirmations *are* working, you begin to put out positive vibes and build momentum, which brings about more and more positive thinking. You will begin to feel a shift in your mindset and you'll build a new resilience that you'll use when hardships come your way.

* * *

Final Thoughts

What are you telling yourself every day? Do you need to rewrite your inner monologue? To help you throughout this process, I've created a downloadable infographic that outlines the 5-step process for writing and using affirmations. You can find it on the Book Resources Page of my website www.ChantalsCreations.com.

What's standing in your way? I encourage you to set aside some time today to get started. Once your affirmations are written, it only takes a few minutes to practice them daily. By being kind and loving to yourself, you'll learn to take charge of your inner monologue and begin to *Create a Life You Love*.

Chapter 6
Make Your Health a Priority

*I believe that the greatest gift you can give
your family and the world is a healthy you.*

~ Joyce Meyer

Having good health is so much more than being
an ideal clothing size. Good health encompasses
physical activity, the foods we consume, our level
of hydration, the amount of sleep we get,
interaction with others, and our overall mental
view of ourselves. For years my self-worth was
attached to a number on a scale and I invested a
significant amount of my time, energy, and
money attempting to reach what, in the scheme
of things, I now see as a fairly insignificant goal.
To be fair, when I slimmed down and others took
notice and doled out the compliments, it felt
good. I enjoyed that, but who wouldn't?
However, the real achievement was waking up
with energy, getting through my day without

feeling the need to consume a gallon of caffeinated beverages, and not having aches and pains in my knees from my body carrying around extra weight. Life is easier when you fuel your body with the right nutrients, get enough sleep, and have regular physical activity or exercise in your daily routine.

It's taken me a few years to put two and two together, but when I follow through with the most basic, commonly known healthy habits and routines, I feel better. I'm able to manage stress better, I have more energy and therefore I'm able to accomplish my daily goals in all areas of my life. I'm generally healthier, so I spend less money on medications and less time in the doctor's office. But it hasn't always been this way.

I've lived all over the world and have never suffered from seasonal allergies the way I do in Kansas. While living here, I routinely get one to three sinus infections a year. In January 2018, I had a particularly rough bout with a terrible sinus infection. I completely lost hearing in my right ear for several months, and a year later, I've still only regained about 85% of my hearing.

At the onset of this sinus infection, I was edging close to my all-time highest weight. I was physically inactive, and I somewhat recklessly ate and drank whatever I wanted whenever I wanted it. It was the height of cold and flu season, and I was unintentionally, but efficiently, doing everything possible to ensure that my immune system was brought down to an all-time low.

Throughout my life, I've always been extremely punctual and have had excellent attendance at school and work. However, this was different. This illness knocked me out for two weeks. My mom drove two hours to take care of me since I could hardly open my eyes or move without vomiting. No matter your age, when you're really sick, you just need your mom.

Over the next few weeks, I slowly recovered and life regained some semblance of normalcy, but I wasn't healthy. My hearing still troubled me and I couldn't handle noisy environments. My vision was still affected by the whole ordeal, so I couldn't drive at night.

The doctors performed a battery of examinations and blood tests. They couldn't determine exactly what was wrong, or make any sort of prognosis, but they did tell me that I was pre-diabetic. This got my attention, and sent me back to my old pattern of negative thinking. I reflected miserably on my situation, and I knew I wanted to make some life changes, but even after all of this, I was still not quite motivated to do anything about it. It was winter and cold outside, I had just gone through a heartbreak, and I was sick! Comfort food and snuggling with my cat was much more appealing than really focusing on starting healthy habits.

Nevertheless, I began making small changes here and there but nothing to write home about. As I was beginning to regain my health and willingness to leave the house for something other than work, my friend Lori invited me to a Party Bus event sponsored by a new local eyeglasses company. As part of the deal, we'd be allowed to pick out free frames as well. I hadn't had my eyes checked in many years, so I needed to update my prescription in order to take advantage of this killer deal. It's funny how you would never imagine the saying, "Everything happens for a reason," being applied to jumping onto a free party bus. However, that party bus may very well have saved my life.

The morning I went in to get my eyes checked, I woke up feeling fine. I was excited to get my new prescription so I could pick up my cute new glasses. I didn't even know that they checked blood pressure at an optometrist's office, but it is a good thing they do. I was surprised when they tested it multiple times, and then brought out a second cuff in case the first one was faulty. After multiple readings with different equipment, the results were the same: my blood pressure was high, at around 208/125. I didn't know much about blood pressure, but the optometrist's reaction was not helping me bring mine down. She asked me several questions about how I was feeling and then carefully watched and listened as I made an appointment with my primary care physician for the same day. She had insisted on this, saying it was that or an ambulance because she was afraid I was on the verge of having a stroke.

When I arrived at my doctor's office, he rechecked my blood pressure, and it was still insanely high. I now know that the normal range is between 90/60 to 140/90, and all of my readings were coming in significantly higher than that. As I was picking up my newly prescribed blood pressure medication, right on cue, my negative thinking took over. All I could think of was that I was freshly single again, I lived alone with my cat, and if I had a stroke over the weekend no one would even notice until Monday when I didn't show up for work.

As with other examples of the lack of self-care, your lack of paying attention to your health will eventually catch up with you. My body had tried to get me to wise up with the serious illness, followed by hearing loss and vision problems, and now I was finally ready to give my own body the full attention it deserved. I didn't want to be a thirty-three year old single woman on blood pressure medication due to my lifestyle choices.

I fully understand that many factors may contribute to a person's elevated blood pressure including genetics, and I have a family history of high blood pressure and cholesterol. However, a mere two months prior I had been in and out of various doctor's offices for my illness and hearing loss, and each time, my blood pressure had not been a concern.

I now had some rather daunting decisions to make. What did I want my future to look like? While none of us is guaranteed a tomorrow, was I willing to knowingly shorten my lifespan? I felt that I had so much more to accomplish, but most importantly to me, my mom doesn't really like cats and my sister is allergic. If I died of a stroke, who would take care of my cat, Ginger? Sadly, I am only partially kidding.

Time to Take Notice

I was still processing how to tackle this issue when my friend Ronda came into work. She reported that she and her daughter had heard good things about a health and wellness program called *Profile by Sanford* and they had made an appointment to ask questions and learn more about it. I was mildly curious but figured I wouldn't be able to afford it. Also, I had been on so many different diet plans over the years and as soon as you go off their meal replacement products, the weight comes right back. However, as Ronda continued to describe the program, I picked up on a few things that appealed to my cynical nature and piqued my interest. She explained that *Profile by Sanford* is a non-profit organization, and their goal is to teach you healthy eating habits. The program is developed to systematically get you off of their food plan and onto your own menus, and participants also receive weekly one-on-one coaching sessions.

I Googled their company's website and started reading reviews from other sources that were not part of their website. By the end of the day, myself and another co-worker, Sarah, had also signed up for what was called a "Discovery Session," a commitment-free opportunity to learn more about the program. All three of us decided to join. As I write this we are eight months in and have lost a combined total of almost 100 pounds.

I think that any health program will work if you follow it. I would encourage anyone to thoroughly investigate several options before choosing one and committing to it. The reason I believe I've been so successful on Profile to this point is that it's easy, my co-workers and I have a built-in support system, and I'm held accountable for my results by the weekly coaching sessions. Honestly, the one-on-one coaching was probably the major attraction of this program. While I've always understood that to lose weight, I need to burn more calories than I consume, and have been armed with that knowledge for decades, I somehow still found myself overweight, pre-diabetic, and on high blood pressure medication.

Time for Changes

I was excited about the program, but was the timing right? It was early May, which is a highly stressful month in the world of educators. Then after that comes summer break, and I really enjoy my summers spent lounging at the pool eating and drinking whatever I please. Maybe I should wait until school begins in August, or perhaps until after the stress of the new semester dies down. But of course then the holidays are right around the corner and who wants to diet then?

Then I remembered that I typically gain about ten pounds every summer. It suddenly occurred to me that if I continued on this path and had a stroke during summer break, it could be weeks before anyone noticed they hadn't heard from me. Clearly, I wanted something to change, but was I willing to make changes? I decided that there would never be a perfect time to start and I needed this to be a lifestyle change, not another fad diet. Regardless of the start time, my health would impact every season of the year for the rest of my life.

What I have learned so far in this journey is that health is multifaceted. In my coaching sessions we target so much more than the number on the scale, what I am eating, and my activity. We discuss hydration, sleep, and realistic expectations. I told my coach it would be hard to get through my birthday week without going off the plan. I was shocked by how they walked me through a judgment-free method of problem-solving, helping me plan a way to stay as close to the program as possible while allowing for real-life circumstances. I was told that this is a marathon, not a sprint. It's not a race to an arbitrary goal weight, followed by celebratory food and drink, and the inevitable steady weight gain after that. That was the old pattern. My new pattern would be to slowly learn new habits along the way as I carefully and intentionally built a newer, healthier me.

Expecting myself to be "perfect" and never again enjoy a cocktail with friends or chips and salsa before a delicious meal was unrealistic. That kind of black and white thinking would inevitably end in failure. Instead of thinking of which items I needed to eliminate from my diet, could I look at it as reducing the number of times I go out to dinner, or the amount of snack foods I consume? Was I willing to make small changes like switching from calorie and carb loaded craft beer to a lighter vodka drink mixed with sparkling water and a flavor enhancer?

As I continued on this journey, more of my friends joined Profile and/or started becoming more aware of their daily health habits. I am a highly social person, and it would be unrealistic to expect myself to only participate in social activities once or twice per month. So my MeetUp group started meeting for walks or bike rides, and I increased my social dancing.

Focusing on my health has helped me learn healthy views and expectations of myself. I have also learned to celebrate the successes rather than condemn myself for my slip-ups. I am no longer in the prediabetic range and am off the blood pressure medication. I have more energy and have an overall more positive outlook on life. It's like Reese Witherspoon's character Elle Woods said in Legally Blonde, "Exercise gives you endorphins. Endorphins make you happy." Regularly and consistently making physical activity and the release of endorphins a part of my daily habits and routines has helped me to **Create a Life I Love**. There are days I am too tired or overwhelmed to follow through with my three-mile walk, but on the days I push through anyway, I'm always thankful that I did. I end up feeling rejuvenated and I'm able to accomplish whatever tasks lie before me with renewed enthusiasm. We will look at how to change our mindsets when feeling tired and overwhelmed in the next chapter.

Your Turn

You may not be in a place where you are able or willing to join a full-on program such as *Profile,* so I will walk you through a few of the basic health principles that have helped me on this journey.

Stay Hydrated

We've all heard that we should drink eights cups of water a day, which translates into sixty-four ounces, but why is this important? Our bodies need water to properly function and to perform tasks such as regulating body temperature, flushing out waste, and lubricating the joints. Studies have shown a direct correlation between levels of stress and adequate hydration. The brain and other organs cannot function properly when dehydrated, so learning to monitor water intake can help reduce feelings of stress.

The specific amount needed can vary person to person based on their activity level, weight, and the temperature of their environment. For example, we need more water when outside working on a hot day than when lounging indoors watching TV. Generally speaking, aiming for eight cups of water per day is a good guideline. I personally don't mind the taste of water, however, I have had many conversations with people who struggle to get in enough water, so here are a few tips that you might find helpful.

1. Plan ahead by carrying water with you

2. Add flavor with the use of calorie-free additives such as Mio

3. Throw in a Powerade Zero or La Croix to switch it up

4. Puree fruits and freeze in ice cube trays to be added to a glass of water

5. Add a squirt of lemon or lime to your water glass or bottle

6. Eat water-rich vegetables such as; cucumber, zucchini, celery, tomatoes, bell peppers, cauliflower or lettuce. Or enjoy water-rich fruits like watermelon, strawberries, cantaloupe, peaches, oranges, and grapefruit.

Get Enough Sleep

The National Sleep Foundation recommends seven to nine hours of sleep for adults ages eighteen to sixty-four. This has been a struggle for me as I am a bit of a night owl. When I get going on a project, I'd rather pull an all-nighter and get it done than worry about getting a good night's sleep. As part of this journey, I decided to commit to at least seven hours of sleep per night on weeknights. When I looked at what time I needed to get up for work the next morning and calculated what time I would need to start my bedtime routine, I felt a bit like an old lady heading to bed by 9:30pm. However, the way I feel the next morning outweighs squeezing in one last episode on Netflix or washing the dishes in the sink before bed. Everything will still be there tomorrow and if I am well rested, I will be better able to tackle it. I thoroughly enjoy looking at my Fitbit stats the next morning to see if I reached my goal.

I do feel the need to add the disclaimer that I am single and don't have children. Scheduling extra hours of sleep may be an unattainable goal for you at your current phase of life. My sister has three children under the age of five, and I'm sure she hasn't had a solid four hours of sleep in at least five years. However, she works hard to practice many of the other healthy habits such as eating well and working out regularly. You'll know best what is a realistic and attainable goal for yourself. Even the smallest positive changes will make a difference. Start where you are and make small improvements over time.

Eat Well

Regardless of your health goals, fueling your body with the proper nutrients can go a long way. For me, my biggest eye-opener has been portion control. We are conditioned through the size of our plates and the servings when we go out to eat to consume much more than we need. As part of my Profile coaching sessions, we look at and discuss what an actual portion size is and I even weigh my foods as I am meal prepping.

The first week it seemed more like rations than dinner, it seemed to be such a small amount of food. However, as my body has adjusted, I realize that eating six small meals throughout the day is much better for me than three large meals. My metabolism keeps going, and I don't crash mid-day like I used to. I have bought smaller bowls and plates and now use my salad forks when eating. When my brain would see a small amount of food on a large plate, it convinced me that I needed more food. Now that it sees a heaping amount of food on a smaller plate, I finish feeling full and satisfied.

It's humorous and remarkable to think about how that small change has made such a big difference. Another trick I've picked up is that if I do eat out with family or friends, I either split a healthy meal or ask for a take-home box early on. If the other half is out of sight, it is out of mind and I can eat it the next day. Almost every restaurant has chicken breast and vegetables, I may have to ask them to hold their signature cheese sauce, but I can usually find something that is not going to make me feel disgusting after I eat it.

There are multiple healthy meal plans out there such as Keto and Paleo. Research them and find the right fit for you based on your lifestyle and taste preferences. Join Facebook groups made up of other people eating similarly to seek encouragement and recipe ideas. There's a saying that you cannot outrun a bad diet, and I have found this to be true. No matter how much I work out, if I consistently make poor eating choices, it will still catch up with me.

Of course, there are times when I throw caution to the wind and eat or drink something unhealthy. But the critical thing to remember is that consistency is what matters. If I go off plan occasionally and pair that decision by having a smaller portion at the next meal and increase my workout over the next couple of days, the plan will still work. The trouble comes if I allow negative "all or nothing" thinking to creep into my mind. If I tell myself that since I strayed from the plan a little bit, I may as well just give up and drop the plan entirely because it doesn't matter anymore. This negative self-talk is why many of us get trapped in the yo-yo diet cycle. Remember the lessons from the previous chapters of this book, and allow yourself grace and kindness as you restate your goals and start again tomorrow.

Activity

The American Heart Association recommends at least 30 minutes of moderate-intensity aerobic exercise on at least five days a week for a total of 150 minutes per week. Or if you are already in decent shape, you could switch that to a minimum of 25 minutes of vigorous aerobic activity at least three days a week for a total of 75 minutes per week. This recommendation poses a few obstacles in my life. First, I don't particularly enjoy working out. Second, I'm busy and have better things to do with my time. Third, I have gym phobia and would rather gouge my eyes out than go to a place where I'll be surrounded by beautiful, fit people at a gym. This, of course, does not stop me from making a financial donation monthly to a gym I have not accessed in over a year.

So what's a girl to do to overcome those obstacles? Well, I found activities that don't need a gym and don't feel like a workout. It is amazing what a good and enjoyable workout I get from Ballroom and Latin dancing. However, the cost of lessons can really add up quickly, so I now stick mainly to social dance opportunities. I also recently moved to a neighborhood that seems to beckon me to be outside exploring it. The neighborhood is surrounded by two rivers and there are many paths and trails that are enjoyable for walking or biking. If I'm alone, I love to listen to an audiobook and take in the beauty around me. I love smiling and nodding at the dozens of other people out enjoying our beautiful neighborhood as we pass each other. There is something communal about the whole experience. It is also easy to drum up someone to join me on these walks and bike rides, which kills two birds with one stone: I get my daily physical activity and my social fix.

I feel guilty even making the "I don't have enough time," excuse. As I mentioned earlier, my sister has three kids under the age of five, and I am pretty sure she is campaigning for *Mom of the Year*. Her level of commitment and dedication to her and her family's health and wellbeing is quite amazing. She recently ran her second half-marathon and briefly held a record at her YMCA on a machine known as *Jacob's Ladder* for sustaining the longest time on it, and she was eight months pregnant with baby number three at the time. It would be so much easier for her to stop working out and just go through a drive-thru every night for dinner, promising that once the kids are older and life settles down, she will get back on track. She is an inspiration to me, and I am a little jealous that I did not get the "running" gene that it seems the rest of my family has. My dad has completed multiple marathons and frequently runs half marathons and 10Ks like it's no big deal. Who knows, maybe after I am done with this book a new bucket list item may replace it on the list, and I will sign up for something longer than a 5K. That's one of the amazing things about this journey. There is no final destination. The more we learn, grow, and experience, the more we feel open to trying and doing the new things that build our healthy lifestyle.

* * *

Final Thoughts

No matter what your current health habits are, we all know the basics of what we're supposed to do. However, many of us fail to consistently follow those basic guidelines. I encourage you to start small and to allow yourself grace and forgiveness when you reach the inevitable slip up. Each day is a new day, so just take it one day at a time. We don't fall into unhealthy habits and gain weight or become pre-diabetic overnight. We cannot realistically expect ourselves to fix the issue overnight. For me, I have had the most success when I schedule my workout plan and post it on my calendar. The schedule encourages me to leave work at a decent hour because I have an important appointment to keep, and that appointment is with myself. I allow some wiggle room from time to time, but I try to remain as consistent as possible.

I highly recommend you use some type of tracking tool to help keep you on target. I personally love the free version of MyFitnessPal.

I have the app on my phone and use it to track my calories and activity. It also links to my Fitbit and together, they help motivate me to stay on track. I've discovered there are days when getting a full, three-mile walk/jog is just not in the cards. On those days, doing a quick ten minutes of activity is better than no activity at all. Be realistic and look at your schedule as you plan your day and your week. Maybe one day you'll be able to fit in three ten-minute sessions rather than one thirty-minute session. The important thing is that you're trying.

Find forms of activity that are enjoyable to you. If you hate running, don't sign up for a half marathon thinking that will motivate you. It might work, but why make yourself miserable along the way? I love taking dance classes and exploring my neighborhood. So I primarily dance and walk, jog, or bike. Think about active things you enjoy or have always wanted to try and start adding those to your schedule. The most important thing is to take a cue from the Nike ads and Just Do It! There's no time like the present, there will never be a better day to feel better, so start now.

Chapter 7
Change Your Mindset, Change Your Life

Nothing can stop the man with the right mental attitude from achieving his goal; nothing on earth can help the man with the wrong mental attitude.

~ Thomas Jefferson

Are you a glass half empty, or a glass half full person? For most of my life, I have had a glass half empty view of the world. When I started down this self-improvement path, I quickly realized how that mentality was inhibiting my growth and my ability to **Create a Life I Love**. Not only was the power of a positive mindset in the majority of the books I was reading, but my own outlook was beginning to change as I started to incorporate the other daily practices and habits recommended. I love the Mark Twain quote, "I have been through some terrible things in my life, some of which actually happened." It really makes me stop and think, when I am having a tough day, how much of the bad day actually happened versus how much of it was bad due to how I was perceiving it?

Have you ever known someone who would fit into the category of a Negative Nellie? After much soul-searching and being honest with myself, I can admit that there have been times in my life when I have fallen into that category. The good news is that I did not have to stay there, and neither does anyone else. The bad news is that the only behavior we can control is our own. So if we recognize the trait in another person, we cannot change it for them or force them to see it within themselves.

This is true for ourselves as well, no one can change our behavior for us. In order to make any type of change, we must have the self-awareness to recognize the issue, and that self-awareness must be matched with a desire to do something about it. I can acknowledge that I am being pessimistic, but unless I decide I want something different and that I am willing to do the work it takes to create new habits, I'll remain stuck right where I am. Take a look at your own journey. If you decide you'd like to change the negative mindset that is blocking you from **Creating a Life You Love**, this is the chapter for you.

My Negative Mindset

I grew up as an Army brat, and we moved every two to three years. It was my common pattern to spend the first several months complaining about the new location. During this time, I would compare it to the old location, remembering it with rose-colored glasses and forgetting that I spent the first several months complaining about that location too. After the adjustment period, I would find things that were OK with the new location, but complained that there was never enough to do, and I was always bored. My mom would tell me that only boring people get bored and point out the many options that were available to me. I didn't want to hear her suggestions or step out of my comfort zone to try anything new. I wanted to stew in my negative mindset. Before long, it was time to move again, and the pattern would repeat itself. Ironically, I would tell my new friends how great the previous place had been and how this new location was so lame.

It didn't matter if we moved to a small town or to a large city. It could be the plains of Kansas or the beaches of Panama, I was stuck in a negative mindset. I was even upset and threatened to emancipate myself from my parents when we moved again during my senior year. Yes, moving during your senior year of high school is not ideal, but we moved to The Netherlands! What an amazing opportunity. Many of my friends were envious of the adventure, yet, I wasted the first several months sulking to the point that my mom took me to a therapist. After meeting with me, his diagnosis was that I had a bad attitude. Further, he stated that he would be of no help to me unless I was the one who wanted to be helped.

As an outsider looking in, my mom could see the bigger picture and wanted to help me break out of this negative mindset. However, I didn't want to help myself. I wanted to wallow and feel sorry for myself. I missed my friends, my high school sweetheart, and the freedoms that came with being able to drive. In Europe, the driving age was 18, so I went from flying down the street in a big blue F-150 truck, affectionately called "Big Blue," to relying on my mom to drive me around. I was not impressed with the demotion, and made sure anyone willing to listen was aware of it.

Wake-Up Call

Everyone old enough to understand what was happening can relive the vivid details of where they were on September 11, 2001. We had been living in The Netherlands for three months after moving from a suburb of Washington D.C where my dad had worked at the Pentagon. I had spent the last three months being an absolute brat and blaming my dad and his job for making us move.

Due to the time difference, it was after school and I was changing for volleyball practice when we were ushered into the gym and informed by our coach what was happening stateside. When we got the news that a plane had hit the Pentagon, it shook me to my core. In that instant, I could see that everything happened for a reason and due to our move, I did not have to fear for my dad's immediate safety. What I had spent so much time and energy being negative about was clearly revealed as a blessing to my family. Don't wait for a tragedy to wake you up; make a choice to work on changing your mindset beginning now.

After my senior year, I ended up in Laramie, Wyoming to pursue my bachelor's degree. Wyoming: the state where sheep outnumber the people and it snows in June. I joke that I experienced more culture shock moving there than I did when moving to any of the multiple countries we had the opportunity to live in. I am not a small town girl and I do not like cold weather, so there was much to complain about. But the price was right, they had the degree I wanted, and extended family was nearby while my immediate family was still in The Netherlands. I made the best of my years there and ended up having a blast.

I then moved from that tiny college town to Wichita, Kansas, and thought I had hit the jackpot. In my eyes, there were endless things to do and places to explore. However, I would meet locals who claimed there was nothing to do. Moving from a town with a population of fewer than 16,000 people, this was mind-boggling. Then I recalled the many times I had a negative mindset about where I had been living. I've come to realize that you can live in the middle of New York City and be bored if you have a negative mindset.

We have an active choice to make. We can hunker down and be miserable for the entire ride, or we can acknowledge that we have one life to live and choose to embrace joy and *Create a Life We Love.*

Changing Your Mindset

I want you to try something. Think to yourself, "I am so stressed out and exhausted. Today is the longest day ever!" How do you feel? I'm willing to bet that regardless of how you were feeling prior to thinking those things, you are now feeling more stressed out and exhausted than you were. Often, having a negative mental attitude happens so naturally, we are not even conscious of it. It takes work to notice that our internal monologue is feeding our subconscious negativity, and it takes even more conscious work to make it stop.

When you catch yourself thinking negatively, reframe your thought. You can do this in the above example by saying something such as, "There is plenty of time to accomplish my priority tasks, I feel energized and ready to tackle them." It may or may not be true, but if you say it and begin to believe it, you will start to notice a change in how you approach your day-to-day stress.

Changing your overall mindset has many similarities to changing your negative self-talk.

They are the same principle, the only difference is that with negative self-talk you are generally focused inward on just yourself. With a negative mindset, you see the whole world with a negative slant. You focus on the flaws of your coworkers and family members rather than appreciating their strengths. You see challenges as stumbling blocks and new experiences as overwhelming or frightening. Instead, we can face new challenges and experiences by viewing them as growth opportunities.

One of the things about maintaining a negative mental attitude is that you attract what you focus on. Your perception truly becomes your reality. If you focus on what you don't like about your job, your spouse, your financial situation, or your life in general, not only will it stay exactly the same, it can get worse! You unintentionally program your brain to seek out more and more negativity. Who wants that?

Influence Your Mindset

Take a few minutes to reflect on the sources of influence you encounter day to day. Consider sources such as the news, social media, and the people with whom you regularly spend time.

What is the positive to the negative ratio that these information sources bring into your life?

The news tends to be overwhelmingly negative, so I choose not to watch it. If you are one who likes to be informed of what is going on in the news, try to limit your exposure or choose news sources that focus on facts rather than exaggerating negativity to increase their ratings. As you scroll through your social media, if there are people who are constantly posting those vague, woe is me posts, unfollow them. In Chapter 9 we will go into the importance of choosing your friends and daily influences wisely. Every positive or negative concept you see or hear influences how negative you feel or how positive you are able to become.

When you do encounter negativity, acknowledge and question it. For example, if you see a news clip about a local homicide and you begin to think about how dangerous the world is these days, tell your brain, "Stop!" Then question, is the world really any more dangerous than it was yesterday? Does this news clip need to impact your feeling of safety and the lens you see the world through? Are there good things going on in your community whether or not the news chooses to give those things equal coverage? Seek sources of positivity to balance or replace the sources of negativity.

I am not saying to become like an ostrich with your head buried in the sand, oblivious to the world around you. I am challenging you to be aware of how negativity affects you and to make conscious decisions to decrease negative influences while increasing positive ones. There are many social media pages you can follow that post daily inspirational and motivational quotes or verses. Follow a few of those pages to ensure there's positivity sprinkled into your daily news feed.

Your Turn

Visualize a scale from 0-10, with 0 being incredibly negative and 10 being so positive that your face hurts from smiling. Throughout your day, assess your thoughts and self-rate where you are. If you find yourself stuck in a negative mindset, here are a few activities that can help you get back on track.

- Acknowledge to yourself that you are focusing on negative thoughts and accept it. If you judge yourself for having the thought, you will begin to focus on beating yourself up and continue with the negativity cycle. Say to yourself that you recognize that your internal monologue is negative and that you are now going to reframe your thoughts.

- Question your thought. For example, if you did not get a promotion you were hoping for and are now thinking to yourself that you will get fired. Ask yourself if that is true, are you really going to lose your job? Then focus on your accomplishments within your career.

- Page through your Gratitude Journal, remembering how you felt when those things happened. Even if you've already spent time today writing out your gratitudes, write down a few more. Focusing on being grateful will help you reset.

- Take a walk, preferably outside and not in an overly urban area. Try to get to a park where you can enjoy the healing effects of nature. The fresh air and the vitamin D from the sun can work wonders for your mental attitude. What do you see, hear, and feel? Drop the headphones for a moment, and focus on the sound of the birds. As you walk, feel the wind on your skin, and see the vivid colors swirling around you.

- Monitor your sources of influence and make a conscious decision to decrease the negative ones and increase the positive ones.

- Seek out ways to help others less fortunate than you. Sometimes we need perspective to get out of our own heads and appreciate the bigger picture.

* * *

Final Thoughts

Having a positive mindset does not necessarily mean you're always going to feel "happy." You might be in an incredibly difficult situation but can still find something positive within it. In the words of Forrest Gump, "Life is like a box of chocolates, you never know what you're gonna get." However, after realizing that the middle of the chocolate is not what you were hoping for....it's still chocolate. Also, there's an entire box of chocolates in front of you. Why waste your time lamenting over the wrong choices you may have made, when you can dig down deep and make a different choice. You can choose a different path, and live a more positive life.

Only you can make that choice, and there may be days you choose not to take the next step. Accept that you are perfectly imperfect and tomorrow is a new day. The important thing is to recognize where you are on the mindset scale and consciously work towards shifting your thoughts over time in order to *Create a Life You Love.*

Access the FREE Mindset Rating Scale to help you identify where you are, by going to the Book Resources Page on www.ChantalsCreations.com.

Chapter 8
Set Goals and Define Clarity

If you don't design your own life plan, chances are you will fall into someone else's plan. And guess what they may have planned for you? NOT much.

~ Jim Rohn

I consider myself a fairly goal-oriented person. I enjoy feeling that I'm working toward something and I feel a sense of purpose and accomplishment through pursuing additional college degrees every couple of years. In fact, I was looking into advanced degree programs to begin working on my Ed.D when I accepted the challenge to write this book. I knew I was ready for a new growth experience, and I'll most likely continue my pursuit of an advanced degree in the next year or so, but I opted to try something completely out of the box this time around.

I'm not sure if it's just my nature, or if being raised as an Army brat somehow influenced my need to continually seek out something new and different every couple of years. I have noticed that while I no longer pack up and move to a different country every two to three years, I do begin to seek out new and exciting challenges around that time frame. I love where I live and my career, so I am not willing to shake up those variables too much. However, I find other ways to learn and grow continually.

Throughout this book so far, I have shared with you how I have tackled various areas of my life in order to **Create a Life I Love**. In this chapter, we will focus specifically on why creating goals is essential, how to successfully navigate past barriers in your way, and how you can create SMART goals.

Becoming Goal-Oriented

By creating goals, you are giving yourself a long-term vision as well as short-term motivation. The practice of creating goals can impact every area of your life, such as your personal growth and development, career, health, finances, or accomplishing special projects that you feel passionate about. I recommend targeting one or two long-term goals to get you started. This will allow you to focus on the successful implementation and completion of the goals. If you bite off more than you can chew, there's a chance you may choke if you haven't learned how to set yourself up for success.

When you are focused on a goal, you are more likely to organize your time in ways that benefit you. You will begin to prioritize your time and intentionally focus on the activities that align with your goals. We all have the same 24 hours in a day, but if you are not goal oriented, you may find that you end up spending a significant amount of those hours on insignificant things such as social media and binge-watching hours of television.

There's a time and place for relaxation, and those things are not inherently wrong. However, I've noticed when I am not focused on a specific goal, suddenly I feel that I don't have enough time to keep up with even the most basic activities such as errands or household chores. Yet my Netflix account history indicates that I somehow had ten spare hours that week to binge on the latest season of some recently released show. When I am goal-oriented and follow the simple practices outlined in this chapter, I actually feel like I have more time on my hands to be productive.

Another reason to create goals is to accomplish our big dreams. Whether you have spent time reflecting on it recently or not, it's likely that there is some big dream deep within you that sparks excitement and creativity, yet feels unattainable. I challenge you to get in touch with your internal dreamer and dream big, not worrying about what it would take to make your dream a reality.

Perhaps you'd like to take a dream vacation, start a business, write a book, or lose a significant amount of weight. No matter what your dream might be, allow yourself to dream it. Spend time visualizing what it will look like and how you will feel when you accomplish this dream. Think of it in this way: If your dream opportunity presented itself today, would you be ready for it? If not, it may be time to define your goal and make a plan to achieve it. There is no time like today. If we put growth off until tomorrow, when an opportunity comes knocking, it will go to someone else.

For example, if I had a dream to be in the symphony orchestra, yet did not set and regularly work towards that goal, when auditions came up,

I wouldn't be ready to perform. A marathon runner begins training long before the actual race. A doctor begins their education long before earning that title. A parent who dreams of putting their child through college set a goal and aligned their behavior years before that first tuition check was due. No matter your goal, pick a start date and move in the direction of your dream.

Managing Your Time

In Steven Covey's book, "The Seven Habits of Highly Effective People," he explains seven habits that can help anyone become more effective and reach their full potential. These seven habits have even been adapted for children and are being taught as part of the *Leader in Me* program in schools around the world. If children as young as five can learn and implement these habits, surely adults can benefit from these lessons. I'd like to spend a moment focusing on two of the recommended habits that can help us learn to set and reach personal goals. They are Habit Number Two, "Begin With the End in Mind" and Habit Number Three, "Put First Things First."

In order to *Begin With The End In Mind*, spend time reflecting on your dreams. What really gets you pumped up and excited? What feels scary because it is out of your comfort zone? Hint, if it scares you, you're probably on the right track.

Think about what that end result will be. Focus on how you will feel when you accomplish your goal and visualize yourself reaching it. Create a personal mission statement or manifesto to read daily. This can be similar to your affirmations created in Chapter 5. Write your goal in the present tense and make it as specific as possible, eliciting the emotions you would feel if you had already accomplished your goal. Once you have the end goal solidified in your mind, we can begin to work backward on the baby steps it will take to get us there.

For Habit Number Three, *Put First Things First*, we'll look at ways to help prioritize your goal and your time. Author John C. Maxwell highly recommends that we plan every day in advance. He states that 1 minute of planning can save 5-10 minutes during the execution of a plan. I've put this practice in place by making a daily to-do list that includes the habits and routines listed in previous chapters of this book. My to-do list includes things such as: reviewing my affirmations, tracking my meals, physical activity and sleep, writing my gratitudes and proof of abundance, and all the tools I've described in this book that bring me a sense of purpose and satisfaction. I also include time to reflect on what I've planned to accomplish that day.

You can incorporate this easy practice as well. All you need is a notebook and a writing utensil. You could also do it electronically, but I find something satisfying in being able to physically check off the items as I complete them. Set aside time in the morning to get your day off on the right foot. This practice allows you time to reflect on your priorities for the day. There may be items that *must* be accomplished that day, and there may be some that may get pushed onto tomorrow or the next day. When we *Put First Things First*, our focus can be on what helps us to meet our overall goal(s), and we can more easily eliminate distractions.

Eliminating Distractions

When it comes to distractions, reflect on your past habits. What are the usual temptations that derail your productivity? What new habits can you put into place to help you move forward? Use that information to create a personal change plan that outlines what you will do to resist, remove, or transform this obstacle. For example, I know every time I get a text or a social media notification, I feel the need to take the time to respond right away, although my personal goal is to write this book. I've set aside the time to write daily, but what can I proactively do to overcome these distractions? This would seem to be an easy problem to resolve since my phone can be switched to "Do Not Disturb" with the click of a button. However, it takes self-control and discipline to follow through, not only by turning my phone to "Do Not Disturb," but to avoid the temptation to constantly check my phone for messages.

Take a few moments to think through what your distractions and obstacles will be and proactively put a plan in place to avoid these pitfalls. If your goal is health-related and you're often tempted to grab fast food on the way home from work because you're too tired to cook, what plan can you incorporate to prevent that from happening? If you set aside time on the weekend to meal plan, grocery shop, and meal prep, on that next busy weeknight, it's actually easier to go home and eat what you've already prepared than it is to stop at a drive-through. The common saying, "If you fail to plan, you plan to fail," is so true when it comes to goal setting. So make a plan and stick to it.

Be Intentional With Your Circle

Another key component to setting yourself up for success is to surround yourself with people who are reaching for their goals with gusto. You want that energy and motivation to rub off on you. You can also get an accountability partner. This is a popular strategy that can sometimes backfire, so choose your person wisely. We've all had, or have been, that workout buddy that convinces the other to skip the workout for just one day. When skipping the workout becomes the norm, the healthy goal dies. Jim Rohn says, "You are the average of the five people you spend the most time with." So choose those five people wisely. We will look at the importance of choosing our friends wisely in the next chapter.

You will want to seek out three types of people:

- Someone who is ahead of you in their journey so you can learn from them

- Someone at your similar level to share growing pains with

- Someone behind you on their journey. If you can teach a skill to someone else, then you can feel confident that you really know it. By spending time giving back and mentoring someone, you will not only be giving back what others have graciously taught you, but you're growing personally as well.

Other Tips

A warning given in the book, "Change Anything" by Kerry Patterson, Joseph Grenny, David Maxfield, Ron McMillan, and Al Switzler, is to beware of the "willpower trap." This is the disappointing cycle that can sometimes trap us, despite our best intentions. First, we make a commitment to change. Then over time we see a decrease in our motivation and inevitably return to our bad habits, until we finally believe we cannot accomplish our goals and we give up.

To combat this negative cycle, follow the guidance throughout this chapter. You can also make your goals public to create a level of accountability; sharing what you're working toward with family, friends and coworkers on social media. You can also develop mini-deadlines; dividing a big goal into smaller, more attainable pieces.

Here are a few things to keep in mind while reaching for your goals. Find ways to maintain balance. Your family, career, and responsibilities should not suffer long-term due to your goal. If anything, these other important areas of your life should be enhanced. While I was focusing on financial goals, I found that I unintentionally lost 12 pounds. I wasn't focusing on health, but due to the discipline and focus I was applying to one area of my life, other areas of my life blossomed as well. Do not forget the importance of self-care as outlined in Chapter One.

Throughout the time you are working toward your goals, it is important to stay consistent. When Jerry Seinfeld decided he wanted to be a comedian, he committed to writing one joke every day. Whether good or bad, he would write one joke per day. What is one thing you can do every day to reach your goal? Maybe you'll set aside the time for at least thirty minutes of physical activity each day, or maybe reading a chapter or two each day from a book related to your field will help you reach a professional or personal goal.

Whatever your goal, decide what daily practice will bring you closer to your goal over time. Jerry Seinfeld made a visual for himself where he would make an X on the calendar for every day he accomplished his mini-goal of writing one joke per day. This simple, visual activity can be put into place for any goal. The more Xs you mark on the calendar, the more you become motivated to avoid breaking the chain.

Remember that you are not alone, and that people are designed to be collaborative. Seek out friends and mentors who may be willing to offer guidance and support. If there is no one available to help you in person, use the technology available to you through sources such as YouTube and online courses. As outlined in Chapter 4, books are an excellent way to expand your knowledge and receive guidance from someone further along on their journey.

No matter what you do, always remember to allow yourself grace. We will inevitably break the chain, miss a deadline, and not follow through with our personal change plan when an obstacle or temptation pops up. We are human, and this is a marathon, not a sprint. The important thing is to get up, dust yourself off, and keep going. Don't beat yourself up or get hung up on a downward emotional spiral. That reaction will only waste more of your time. Instead, revise your plan and deadlines as needed, and keep moving. You were the one who created these goals in the first place, no one else is going to be upset if you change your plans to better fit your needs as you learn, grow, and get through life as it happens.

It is essential to select tangible, attainable goals, and to take the time to celebrate your successes. If you shared your mini goals publicly, celebrate publicly. If your healthy living goal is to lose 50 pounds, maybe you'll decide to set mini goals and take time to celebrate when you reach them. Perhaps you'll celebrate for every 10 pounds lost by buying a new workout outfit.

Your Turn

A great way to set up your goals is by using the SMART goals system. The original version of this system was introduced in the 1950s by author Peter Drucker in his book, *"The Practice of Management."* This system is still in use today, because it's a practical way to help you set concrete, actionable steps towards reaching your goals. Below we will walk through examples of SMART goals that align with the healthy habits and routines we have covered throughout the book.

SMART Goal

S—Specific: Be clear about your goal

M—Measurable: What or how much do you want to accomplish

A—Attainable: Set realistic goals that work for you

R—Relevant: Set goals that are meaningful in your life

T—Timely: Set a practical time-frame for reaching your goal

Example: Practice Self-Care

Specific: I will practice self-care activities

Measurable: by using an activity from Chapter 1: *Make You a Priority*

Attainable: at least one time per day

Relevant: This is important to me so that I can be the best version of myself for my family, friends, and coworkers

Timely: I will do this for four weeks and then review my progress and adjust my goal accordingly.

Example: Practice Gratitude

Specific: I will practice being grateful

Measurable: by writing down at least three gratitudes

Attainable: daily in my gratitude journal

Relevant: This is important to me so that I can reflect on the many blessings I have and shift my mindset to focusing on the positive things in my life

Timely: I will do this for one month and then review my progress and adjust my goal accordingly.

Example: Get Out of Your Comfort Zone

Specific: I will get out of my comfort zone

Measureable: by trying something new

Attainable: at least one time per week

Relevant: This is important to me so that I can Create a Life I Love

Timely: I will do this for one month and then review my progress and adjust my goal accordingly.

Example: Grow in my personal development through reading

Specific: I will increase my reading of non-fiction books

Measureable: by reading or listening to an audiobook at least 30 minutes a day

Attainable: on at least 5 days a week

Relevant: This is important to me so that I can grow personally

Timely: I will do this for one month and then review my progress and adjust my goal accordingly.

Example: Practice Affirmations

Specific: I will practice my affirmations

Measurable: by stating positive affirmations at least five minutes daily

Attainable: every morning before leaving my house for the day

Relevant: This is important to me so that I can replace my negative self-talk

Timely: I will do this for one month and then review my progress and adjust my goal accordingly.

Example: Increase healthy activity

Specific: I will increase my activity

Measurable: by participating in at least 30 minutes of physical activity, as logged on my Fitbit activity tracker

Attainable: on at least 5 days a week for a total of 150 minutes per week

Relevant: This is important to me so that I can increase my energy level and overall fitness

Timely: I will do this for four weeks and then review my progress and adjust my goal accordingly.

* * *

Final Thoughts

You can use these examples as a guide to create your own SMART goals. Remember to choose one or two goals to tackle at a time and to allow yourself grace on the days you don't get to your goal. *Creating a Life You Love* is a long-term goal and does not happen overnight. We learn just as much from our valleys and mistakes as we do from our peaks and successes.

Remember that this is an ongoing process; so continually review, update, and adjust. Once you're ready, set a new goal. Our life is a journey and the minute we decide to stop learning, growing, and challenging ourselves, we become complacent. Take time to appreciate where you are and live in the moment, but then look ahead to where you want to be in six months, one year and five years. What will your life look like when you're setting achievable goals, reaching for healthy habits, and intentionally *Creating a Life You Love*?

Access a FREE "Don't Break the Chain" resource to track your daily progress towards your goals on the Book Resources Page on my website at www.ChantalsCreations.com.

Chapter 9
Choose Your Friends Wisely

Surround yourself with the dreamers, and the doers, the believers, and thinkers, but most of all, surround yourself with those who see the greatness within you, even when you don't see it yourself.

~ Edmund Lee

When I was growing up, my parents taught me to choose my friends wisely. For the most part, my friends were kids we knew through church and other military families, so things were fairly simple. However, once you grow up and are out of the shadow of your parent' protection, they hope you have internalized important lessons such as this. I tend to be naive and believe that people are generally good, even after they have repeatedly shown me otherwise. Nevertheless, this lesson has helped me on my journey, and I hope it will be beneficial to you as well.

Think about your inner circle of friends. Do their life goals mirror yours? Do their health habits align with your health habits? My good friend Melissa commonly says, "Like attracts like." Meaning that generally speaking, if you are surrounded by good people, it's likely you are a good person too. When dating, it can be very eye opening if your new prospect has very few people in their life, or if their circle of friends seem shady. Go ahead and mark that down as a red flag and proceed with caution, if you decide to proceed at all.

If it is commonly known that we become like those we associate with, do we want to spend that time with positive or negative people? I know if I spend time with a "Debbie Downer," my old habits come flaring back up and it's difficult to avoid succumbing to the negativity. I also know that if I am doing well on a health and exercise plan, it is in my favor to be purposeful in selecting friends with whom I spend my extra time. It's important to find the friends willing to go on a walk or bike ride and to limit my time with the friends who want to go out for drinks and dinner multiple nights a week.

Why is this Critical?

The people surrounding you influence your thoughts and actions. Surround yourself with motivated high achievers, and you are more likely to be successful. Choose people who push and motivate you to be the best version of yourself. Pair up with people who spark ideas and creativity within you. Consider their activities and goals. Do they align with yours?

My friend, Megan, is a nurse practitioner. Our career fields are different, yet we were both go-getters and high achievers in our early twenties, particularly when it came to seeking higher education and advanced degrees. We had similar viewpoints when it came to work ethic and pushing ourselves to reach our goals. We supported each other and did not guilt one another into slacking off if there was a large project that needed our attention. However, don't be confused here; our personalities aligned in other areas too, and we had plenty of fun-filled nights out on the town. We were just able to prioritize and always made sure to put *First things First* prior to *Sharpening the Saw*, as Steven Covey would say. We also studied Dave Ramsey's, *Financial Peace University* and were intense little debt-paying gazelles. Megan was also my workout buddy for many years. Find people in your world that best match your intentions and goals, and life will be easier and more fun.

Toxic Friends

On the flip side, we all occasionally find a toxic relationship from which we need to cut ourselves loose. This can be very challenging and painful for both people involved in the relationship. However, if you find yourself continually influenced in a negative way that distracts you from your goals, or if the same person continually has no regard for your feelings or how their actions impact you, it might be time to cut them loose. If it is a friendship, over time you may find that you hang out less and less. This can happen in previously healthy friendships too, but perhaps one or both of you have neglected the friendship. I'm speaking specifically of those friendships you know you need to cut loose simply because they have run to the end of their natural course.

In an ideal world, you would be able to bring those past friends up to your level and you could *Create a Life You Love* together. However, that does not seem to be the norm. It is like the old "rotten apple" expression. If you put one rotten apple in a basket of ripe apples, the ripe ones don't make the rotten one ripe. Instead, they all rot. Both people have to want something better and both must be willing to work for it.

When we have to cut a toxic friendship loose, it is not simply that they are not in the same place we are, but often they may be holding us back from growing into a better version of ourselves. Unfortunately, they may feel threatened by the thought of changing old patterns, and actively attempt to sabotage us. Ultimately, you have to take responsibility for your own actions and the direction you want your life to go.

Think about it in this extreme situation. If you were an alcoholic, would you keep the same friends and activities? Hopefully not, because you most likely spent a significant amount of your time drinking with other alcoholics. Our environment and surroundings have a significant impact on our level of success, and part of *Creating a Life You Love* is taking a hard look at every aspect of your life today, then potentially making changes that include which friends you will surround yourself with tomorrow.

This is not to say that everyone in your life should be cut loose if they don't exactly match your interests and goals. As we learned in previous chapters, I believe you should seek people who are ahead of you in your goals so they might help you, those who are where you are today so you can support each other, and those who are behind you in the journey so you can be a source of encouragement to them. There will be important, meaningful people in your life that have nothing to do with your goals but still add value to your life and you will add value to theirs. What I am speaking of in this section, is cutting those people out who do not add value and who actively bring you down. Hopefully, you will not have to face that tough decision, but understand that it may sometimes be necessary.

Toxic Romantic Relationships

I am not sure which is more difficult: ending a friendship or ending a romantic relationship. It most likely varies situation to situation. Your friendships and relationships should add value and lift you up. If they are continually dragging you down, it may be time to let go. In the previous section, I spoke of recognizing when it may be time to let go of a toxic friendship. I will now address recognizing and ending toxic romantic relationships.

When I got married, I didn't "believe in" divorce. When my marriage turned toxic, I believed that I had taken vows and the only choice I had was to follow the "til death do us part" section of our vows. That is not normal or healthy thinking! However, I had been raised with religious convictions and a deep, somewhat instinctive respect for rules. Possible solutions or options escaped me, and I truly felt trapped in the relationship. I didn't know where to turn or what to do about this dangerous situation.

I believed that if I were to ask for help, it would be twisted back against me. I had no idea that my closest family and friends suspected things were not OK. They were patiently waiting for me to reach out to them first, out of fear that if they initiated even the most casual discussion, I would go on the defensive or worse, retreat in anger and they would never hear from me again.

This was an extreme case, but unfortunately, many of my dating relationships prior to my marriage were toxic as well. I had a pattern of co-dependency and habitually chose guys who were unable to commit. I was focused on finding someone to "complete" me and failed to realize that I needed to be a whole person all on my own before I could ever hope to find someone who "complimented" me. A guy I dated in college tried to explain this to me, but I was unable to understand the concept at the time.

I now see that if a relationship, whether friendly or romantic, does not add value to both lives, it's not a healthy relationship, and I'd be better off without it. It took time, but I'm more satisfied and happy being single and reaching for my personal goals than I was when I was tied to someone who didn't share my goals. At the end of the day, although it was difficult to realize; we didn't add value to each other's lives. I am hopeful that when the time is right, I will meet a partner who is equally motivated by their goals and we can support each other as we both live lives we love. Learning to be content while being single was a hard lesson for me, but one that was vital to my journey.

You are meant for amazing things and deserve to be loved and treated kindly. If there is anyone in your life violating this basic right, seek help. I was blessed to have an amazing support system and know I would've been unsuccessful without them. If you are in danger, call 911 or the

National Domestic Violence Hotline at 1-800-799-7233.

Your Turn

Now that you've learned how to identify healthy habits, take some time to chose which ones you'd like to incorporate into your daily routine. Once you have done that, you can write your SMART goals for how to reach them. Then you'll be ready to embark on this amazing journey. If there is someone toxic in your life that you need to distance yourself from, put those measures in place. You can also begin to seek like-minded people through local and online groups that align with your new goals. This may be out of your comfort zone, but that's a good thing. Lean into it and start building a network of influencers around you that push and motivate you to *Create a Life You Love*.

Try this exercise:

1. Write out the top one to three important relationships in your life, the people you know you could call at 3 a.m. and they would be there no matter what. You might not talk daily or see each other in person,

but identify those people on a piece of paper.

2. Reflect on how these important people have added value to your life and how you have added value to theirs.

3. Write down the reasons you are grateful for these relationships.

4. Plan to share your goals with them.

You have now intentionally identified your primary support system. These are the people that when you have your SMART goals written, they will support and love you as you **Create a Life You Love**. The important thing to do now is to get started and be consistent. It's difficult to make life-changing progress on goals that you only work on sporadically. However, as with everything, allow yourself grace as you find the right balance for yourself.

* * *

Final Thoughts

While reflecting on your support system, there may be goals you want to work on that no one in your current support system can help you with.

While they can still be supportive, they might be unable to mentor you or walk alongside you on your journey. In my previous example in *Chapter 2, Bust Out of Your Comfort Zone*, I shared how I wanted to learn to salsa dance. No one in my current circle knew how or where to accomplish that, nor did they have any interest in joining me on the adventure. They were supportive and encouraged me to go after my goal, but I had to expand my circle myself.

You can also expand your circle by getting connected with new friends and like-minded people. If you are interested in:

- Learning to Dance—Get online and search local dance studios. Have fun and just go for it!

- Writing and Self-publishing a Book— Check out Self-Publishing School at http://bit.ly/2RclKrB

- Getting More Fit and Active—Check out your local gym, MeetUps that focus on healthy lifestyles, social media groups that get together for walking or running, etc.

- Starting a Business—Find local entre-preneur Meetups and other social media groups

- Becoming a Speaker—Check out your local chapter of ToastMasters at their website www.toastmasters.org

My mission is to build an active and encouraging community of people striving to **_Create a Life You Love._**

Join the conversation and check out the Book Resources Page on www.ChantalsCreations.com to help you on your journey.

Chapter 10
Own Your Story and Emotions

"Owning our story can be hard but not nearly as difficult as spending our lives running from it. Only when we are brave enough to explore the darkness will we discover the infinite power of our light."

~ Brene Brown

Owning our story and emotions can be the most challenging section of the journey to **Create a Life You Love**. We live in a society where we are taught that "real" men don't cry and if a woman expresses her feelings she is labeled "crazy," or "emotional." We all run around with fake smiles plastered on our faces, and when someone asks how we are, we robotically respond, "Good, you?" What would the world look like if we took a deep breath and dared to respond authentically, with genuine feeling?

Brene Brown is a research professor, author, and TED Talk presenter who has dedicated her career to researching and studying courage, vulnerability, shame, and empathy. As I shared in Chapter 4, when I first stumbled across her work, a few of the thoughts running through my head sounded a bit like this, *"Own my story? Who is this Brene Brown and why would she say that? She doesn't know me or my story. Her story must be prettier and easier to own."* I continued to listen to her audiobook, enjoyed it, and even downloaded a second one, but I was still not ready to put her message into practice.

A few years later, I was on an eight-hour road trip and decided it would be good use of my time to listen to audiobooks. **One of the many books I read on that trip was called "Loving What Is," by Byron Katie.** She takes her readers through a four-step questioning process that helps to reframe negative situations that are holding them back, she calls this process "The Work."

"Loving What Is," challenged my views of my own life experiences, and I'll admit, there were times when I was downright angry with what she was saying. She has her own story of triumph and is helping others by sharing it. However, her approach sometimes made me shut the audiobook off so I could drive without having an emotional breakdown. Once I worked past those emotions, I wondered why it was such a trigger for me. I had spent so long pretending I was strong and had overcome my past. However, I had not really embraced my past or allowed myself to heal.

A Hard Look in the Mirror

I still harbored significant anger regarding my experience during my brief marriage. I was taking very little personal responsibility, yet, I was not one hundred percent innocent in the scenario of our failed marriage. I made the decision to create an online dating account, and I then made the decision to accept a message from someone even though he didn't meet my criteria. I also chose to ignore the red flags presented during our dating phase. Driven by the strong desire to get married and have children by the age of thirty, I blocked out what my gut instincts were screaming at me. I allowed things to move quickly, telling myself I was taking a leap of faith and it was wildly romantic. Hint: If someone or something seems too good to be true, it probably is. Stop, take a step back and re-analyze the situation.

Even on an evening prior to my wedding when things got physical for one of the first times, I literally packed a bag and drove to a nearby hotel. I told myself I was going to call my mom and tell her everything, and that my parents would somehow help me figure out this mess I had created.

On the drive to the hotel though, the shame and embarrassment of admitting how foolish I had been overwhelmed me. Then came the logistical realization that I had moved to another state and was at the beginning of a year-long teaching contract. This particular state has awful education funding, and I had taken a substantial pay cut in order to move to our new home. I knew I couldn't afford to live alone and also couldn't get out of the remaining seven months of my teaching contract. Even if I could, I had given up my dream job and dream house back home. What would I have waiting for me if I returned home?

As all of these frightening and intimidating thoughts were running through my head, he was calling and apologizing. He promised that it was just the stress of our upcoming wedding and promised that in a couple of weeks, once the wedding was behind us, everything would settle down. Like a predictable Lifetime Network Movie character, I dutifully and willingly returned. However, the wedding didn't make the abuse stop and in fact, it only increased in frequency and intensity over the next seven months while we were legally married.

Once I returned to my family and support system back in Kansas and got through the initial shock, I went through the motions of starting my life over again. I was safe, happy, and thankful, but difficult times followed. Holidays and certain dates made my emotions go wonky and I would get angry at myself for not being constantly happy and grateful for all of my many blessings. Finally, I had an epiphany, and I could almost see one of those huge, cartoon light bulbs going off over my head. I began recalling Brene Brown's words, and I began to see how those lessons connected to Byron Katie's four questions in *The Work*. I was finally at a place where I could step back and analyze the bigger picture.

It was as if a heavy veil of shame and self-hatred was finally being lifted from my eyes. While I was working so hard to learn how to be positive and grateful, was there room for authentic feelings that included things such as anger? Or more importantly, could that anger help lead me to forgiveness and closure? But how could I ever get closure from something I was so ashamed of and for which I had worked so hard to over-compensate? I was in a perplexed state but was finally beginning to see that twinkle of light at the end of the tunnel. Clarity and focus were beginning to peek through the dense fog in which I had been so comfortably, if somewhat reluctantly, living.

Your Turn

So what does this mean for you? What feelings and emotions are you not owning? Many people self-medicate through unhealthy habits such as alcohol, drugs, food, or sex. It's also common for people to hide behind the TV or online video games. Why are we turning to those things? Are they helpful or destructive patterns in our lives? What would happen if we were honest about our feelings, accepted them, and then sought healthy ways to cope?

Here is a challenge for you. Take some time to reflect on your life and situation. Forget that we're all supposed to be rockstars with unlimited time and energy. Forget that society tells you that you can "have it all" and be the perfect 1950s housewife while still having a powerful career.

Maybe you can do all these things, but on a day when you feel tired and defeated ... that's OK. When you are overcome by stress and break down in self-pity, that's OK too.

What's not OK is bottling up those emotions and stuffing them down, hiding them from those who want to love and support you. The stress we put on ourselves to be everything to everyone is not sustainable. We were not created to be solo creatures, powering through life alone.

Use the following steps to help guide you as you reflect on how you can move closer toward owning your story and emotions.

1. Reflect on who your team is. Who is your support system? Perhaps it is a friend, coworker, or your spouse. Perhaps you are blessed enough to have a couple of people in mind. Imagine that right at this moment, they're feeling stuck in a negative mindset, the way you sometimes feel. Would you want them to bottle it up and push through it, or would you hope they'd give you a call because you want to be there for them if they have a problem or need someone to vent to for a moment?

We tend to be more forgiving of others than we are of ourselves, so sometimes it helps to reframe our situation by stepping back and trying to look at it from the outside. When we are drowning in a pool of bottled up stress and emotion, this is very hard to do. That is when a good support system can come in handy.

My best friend Melissa is that person for me. She has been with me through all of my ups and downs over our 11-year friendship. She is the one who after visiting me for my thirtieth birthday, looked me in the eye and said she could not leave me there. The previous night I had confided in her about the abuse that I had been trying so hard to cover up for the previous nine months.

2. Feel your feelings. When the holiday season approaches, and I'm floundering; consumed with an anger and sadness that I can't explain because everything in my life seems to be going so well, Melissa is the one who reminds me that this is the time of year I got married. She gently reminds me that it is OK to feel my feelings. By acknowledging these ferociously negative thoughts, they lose some of their power. I can then use reason and logic to help get through the funk. I can use healthy habits and routines rather than turning to unhealthy vices.

3. Allow yourself time to be in the valleys. "Life is too short to be anything but happy." While I love that quote, it's naive to think other valid emotions will not creep in. Life is beautiful, yet frequently messy. There are emotional peaks and valleys. Yes, life is short, and I choose to be happy for most of it. However, there are appropriate times in life for things such as grieving. By not allowing ourselves to feel the valleys, we cannot fully enjoy the peaks. Please notice, I said there is a time for valley emotions. Don't allow negativity to take over your life. Don't get stuck in the valley. Use the healthy habits and routines in this book to help you, and by all means, phone a friend.

4. Recognize that it takes time to own your story and emotions. A few years ago I was approached by a friend who is passionate about raising the awareness of domestic violence. Every year in October she participates in an annual fundraiser for Domestic Violence Awareness Month. She was working on a t-shirt design and wanted quotes from survivors on the back that could be empowering to others suffering in silence. I desperately wanted to support her and this important cause. I wanted to bravely "own my story" but I wasn't ready to share this information with the world at the time.

I submitted the verse Jeremiah 29:11 which says, "For I know the plans I have for you," declares the Lord, "plans to prosper you and not to harm you, plans to give you hope and a future." It had been so helpful to me and had given me hope throughout my experience. However, I was worried that since Wichita seems to be the smallest big city in the universe, and the name Chantal is not one you see every day, someone would see my name and *know it was me*. To me, *knowing* would inevitably lead to *judging*. So instead of having her put my first name next to the verse, I had her put my initials, C.C.

Now every time I wear that shirt, I am proud to be a survivor, but also saddened. I'm saddened that I was unable to own my story for fear of judgment. What if someone who knew me but didn't know my story was suffering in silence? What if they had seen my name on a stranger's shirt at the grocery store? What if I had missed the opportunity to provide the encouragement they needed to reach out for help?

5. Allow yourself grace. Back then, I wasn't at a point where I could post my first name on a t-shirt. Yet today I'm writing a book about my story, which includes that blip in my past. *Creating a Life You Love* is not all sunshine and butterflies, and you will not attain it in a short period of time. There will be days you fall and scrape your knee and ego. Allow yourself grace, laugh at yourself, and keep going.

6. Analyze and grow from your emotions. That t-shirt is a piece of my journey. I could have quickly moved on and not taken the time to reflect on the emotions it brought up. I could have forced them down, refusing to think any further about them. By reflecting and analyzing the emotions of shame it brought up, I was able to make the conscious decision that I was finally done hiding. I wouldn't live in an emotional prison of shame created by my own insecurities.

7. Be generous with your story. Once you're able to own your story, or even a piece of it, use it to help others. You don't necessarily have to write a book about it, but when you see someone going through a similar situation, be there for them, listen empathically, and show patience and kindness. If the time is appropriate, and they seem ready to listen, share your story with them. Sometimes we just need a beacon of light in our darkness to know that we can survive what we are going through.

Over the years as I have processed this particular section of my story, I have been amazed at the strong, intelligent women that I respect who have bravely shared their similar experiences with me. Seeing how they moved beyond their negative experiences, what they've accomplished and achieved since then, gave me hope. My future did not have to be stunted by this small piece of my journey. Who can your story help?

8. Get started. There is no time like the present. Just because you start does not mean you'll reach the finish line on the same day. Start small, share your story authentically and vulnerably with a trusted friend. When you are feeling an emotion, name it. Say out loud, "I am frustrated." Or whatever feeling you are feeling that you might be tempted to withhold. After you acknowledge it, try to pinpoint why this negative emotion was raised to the surface. It might be as easy as, "I am frustrated because I feel like I cannot get ahead, I am constantly playing catch up. It's exhausting!"

Once it's out and acknowledged, you can deal with it. When we waste our energy on hiding from our feelings, we are like hamsters on a wheel. We're running fast but getting nowhere. Are you ready to embrace your story and emotions completely, even the times when your story isn't filled with happiness and overwhelming positivity?

* * *

Final Thoughts

You may not be ready to tackle this step yet, that's why this is the last chapter. You've read about nine other healthy habits and routines that you can focus on before you try this. However, don't forget to revisit this idea from time to time.

You can access a FREE resource to help remind yourself of the steps to Own Your Story on the Book Resources Page on my website located at www.ChantalsCreations.com.

Today may be the day you're just grateful to have survived your story so far. Or maybe this is the day to *Bust Out of Your Comfort Zone*. Wherever you are in your journey, and no matter how amazing a life you're creating, if you slip back into old habits and routines, allow yourself grace and reflect on the "why?" of your story. Why did you begin your journey? What have you learned? Then decide to get back up and keep moving forward on the path to ***Create a Life You Love***.

Create a Life You Love

I hope that you have not only enjoyed this book but that you've also gained practical tips and insights into how to ***Create a Life You Love***. I do believe that everything happens for a reason, and I know that I've been helped in my personal journey through the encouraging words from others who were willing to share their stories. It is my hope that through this book, my story will help at least one person. No matter where you are in your story or journey, the healthy habits outlined in this book can work wonders.

Together, we have walked through 10 practical habits and routines, which all came with action items specifically designed to assist you on this journey. With each step, we considered the importance of being consistent, allowing ourselves grace, and getting started.

Let's recap what the steps are:

1. Make YOU a Priority—Take time to practice self-care

2. Be Grateful—Set aside time to reflect on gratitude

3. Bust Out of Your Comfort Zone—Do things that challenge you

4. Expand Your Mind Through Reading—Make it a habit to read daily

5. Replace Negative Self-talk—Write and practice positive affirmation statements

6. Make Your Health a Priority—Stay hydrated, eat well, get plenty of sleep and regular physical activity

7. Change Your Mindset, Change Your Life—Choose a positive mental attitude

8. Set Goals and Define Clarity—Use the SMART formula to put these habits into action

9. Choose Your Friends Wisely—Surround yourself with positive influences

10. Own Your Story and Emotions—
    Embrace your valleys and turn them
    into growth opportunities

* * *

Final Thoughts

These steps alone did not save me. They were a large part of how I regained control of my life and made a significant, positive difference. However, it is my faith that helps me to maintain underlying feelings of peace, hope, and joy no matter what valley I am in. As I mentioned earlier, the saying in my head during my brief marriage that kept replaying was the verse Jeremiah 29:11, "For I know the plans I have for you," declares the Lord, "plans to prosper you and not to harm you, plans to give you hope and a future." No matter how tough things got, deep down I knew that God did not want this for me. This was not the end of my story.

After leaning heavily on my amazing support system consisting of close family and friends, I was able to begin to see hope again. By implementing the healthy habits and routines outlined, I was able to turn my life around. I am so excited to see where my personal development will take me in the next three to five years. I know I'm on a path moving forward, which I cannot do without accepting and learning from my past.

I don't know your story or where you are on your journey. However, I do know that you are the only you there is, and you are wonderfully amazing in every way. This message gets lost in the shuffle of our busy day to day lives, but it's vital to our success when beginning to *Create a Life We Love*. There's no time like the present, for we are not guaranteed tomorrow.

I invite you to become a member of the *Create a Life You Love* community, where we can encourage each other as we put these practices into place. Let's support each other through the valleys and celebrate together when we reach the peaks. Join the conversation on the Chantal's Creations Facebook Page and share how you are *Creating a Life You Love.*

Resources

For Chapter 2

Emmons RA, et al. "Counting Blessings Versus Burdens: An Experimental Investigation of Gratitude and Subjective Well-Being in Daily Life," Journal of Personality and Social Psychology (Feb. 2003): Vol. 84, No. 2, pp. 377–89.

Zahn, Roland et al. "The Neural Basis of Human Social Values: Evidence from Functional MRI." Cerebral Cortex (New York, NY) 19.2 (2009): 276–283. PMC. Web. 16 Sept. 2018.

Korb, Alex. The Upward Spiral: Using Neuroscience to Reverse the Course of Depression One Small Change at a Time. N.p.: New Harbinger, 2015.

For Chapter 4

Kane, Libby. "9 Things Rich People Do and Don't Do Every Day." Business Insider, Business Insider, 26 June 2014, www.businessinsider.com/rich-people-daily-habits-2014-6.

Merle, Andrew. "The Reading Habits of Ultra-Successful People." The Huffington Post, TheHuffingtonPost.com, 7 Dec. 2017, www.huffingtonpost.com/andrew-merle/the-reading-habits-of-ult_b_9688130.html.

Acknowledgments

To my amazing family, thank you for your ongoing support and encouragement throughout all of the adventures I embark on. You have stood by me through multiple advanced degrees, my emotional peaks and valleys, and the process of writing this book. Dad, thank you for teaching me the importance of generosity, discipline, and for being our family's spiritual leader. Mom, thank you for showing me what it means to be a woman of strength. Michelle and Trevor, thank you for opening your home to me during my difficult divorce, for your ongoing support, and for raising my niece and nephews in a home full of love and laughter.

To Melissa and Ashley, thank you for sharing your strength and bravery during our unforgettable and unplanned escape mission. I do not know where my story would have gone without your support that day. We truly are bonded for life.

To Terri, thank you for your on-going support and encouragement. You are such a wonderful cheerleader!

To the rest of my supportive and wonderful friends, without the breaks filled with laughter and memories, this journey would not be worth embarking on.

To Linda who graciously offered to read through my manuscript, your attention to detail and talent for proofreading has helped transform my ramblings into what I hope is now a helpful resource for others.

To my Launch Team, thank you for generously giving of your time to read and review this book. Your support throughout the self-publishing process helped motivate me to get to the finish line of this project.

To my book team: editor Donna, formatter Debbie, cover designer Angie, and book coach RE Vance, your support and encouragement along with your willingness to share your skills and knowledge helped make this dream a reality. I truly could not have reached this point without each of you.

To you, the reader, thank you for opening yourself up to these words from an imperfect, first-time author. Together, we can change the world by first working on ourselves.

Create a Life You Love,
Chantal

www.ChantalsCreations.com

About the Author

Chantal Cox is a special educator currently serving as an Instructional Coach. She has experienced first hand how the stresses of life can take a toll on your physical and mental health and strives to teach others ways to find a healthy, balanced life. Through her book, YouTube channel, and blog, she shares with authenticity and vulnerability how to implement practical habits and routines to ***Create a Life You Lov***e.

Join her on this incredible journey by visiting her website at www.ChantalsCreations.com.

Last Words

Thank you for reading! I hope this book has helped inspire you to ***Create a Life you Love.*** If you have enjoyed this book, please take 1 quick minute to leave a review on Amazon. This will help Amazon know that you liked the book in order to determine who to recommend it to.

Each review also helps future readers when deciding which of the many wonderful books out there to read next.

If you think I could add value to you, your organization, or your community, please contact me regarding speaking at your next event at Chantal@chantalscreations.com.

Be sure to grab your free companion resources on the Book Resources Page on www.ChantalsCreations.com.

Welcome to this amazing journey,
Chantal Cox, MAEd
www.ChantalsCreations.com

IS WRITING A BOOK PART OF YOUR JOURNEY TO CREATE A LIFE YOU LOVE?

NOW IT'S YOUR TURN

Discover the EXACT 3-step blueprint you need to become a bestselling author in 3 months.

Self-Publishing School helped me, and now I want them to help you with this FREE WEBINAR!

Even if you're busy, bad at writing, or don't know where to start, you CAN write a bestseller and build your best life.

With tools and experience across a variety niches and professions, Self-Publishing School is the only resource you need to take your book to the finish line!

DON'T WAIT

Watch this FREE WEBINAR now, and
Say "YES" to becoming a bestseller:
http://bit.ly/2RclKrB